D0934701

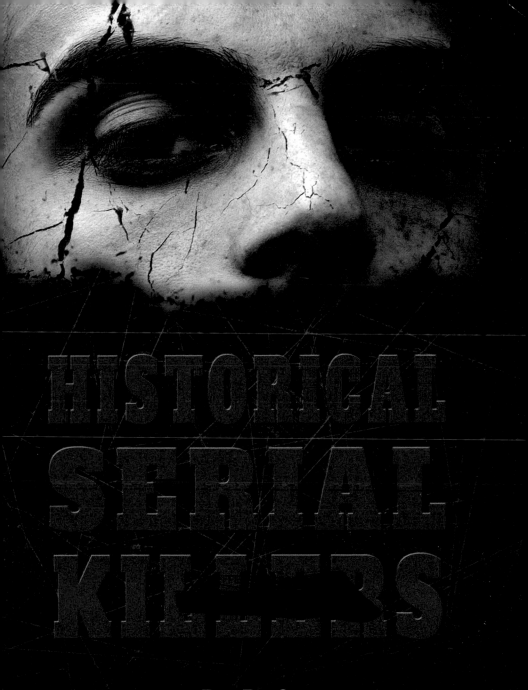

HISTORICAL SERIAL KILLERS

Don Rauf

Enslow Publishing

101 W. 23rd Street
Suite 240
New York, NY 10011
USA

enslow.com

Published in 2016 by Enslow Publishing, LLC.
101 W. 23rd Street, Suite 240, New York, NY 10011

Library of Congress Cataloging-in-Publication Data

Names: Rauf, Don.
Title: Historical serial killers / Don Rauf.
Description: New York : Enslow Publishing, 2016 | Series: The psychology of serial killers |
Includes bibliographical references and index.
Identifiers: ISBN 9780766072909 (library bound)
Subjects: LCSH: Serial murderers--History--Juvenile literature.
Classification: LCC HV6515.R285 2016 | DDC 364.15'23--dc23

Printed in the United States of America

To Our Readers: We have done our best to make sure all websites in this book were active
and appropriate when we went to press. However, the author and the publisher have no
control over and assume no liability for the material available on those websites or on
any websites they may link to. Any comments or suggestions can be sent by e-mail to
customerservice@enslow.com.

Contents

Dexter (2006–2013) told the story of a blood spatter analyst in Miami who also happened to be a serial killer. Dexter (played by Michael C. Hall, right) killed only people he **deemed** morally reprehensible.

Movies and television shows have no shortage of serial killers. Some of the more famous ones are Anthony Hopkins as Hannibal Lecter in *Silence of the Lambs*, Kevin Spacey as John Doe in *Seven*, Christian Bale as Patrick Bateman in *American Psycho*, and Barry Foster who plays Robert Rusk, the serial killer in Alfred Hitchcock's *Frenzy*. Serial killing in real life is horrible and deadly serious, but sometimes the media plays the idea for laughs: The two old ladies in the Cary Grant movie *Arsenic and Old Lace* are serial killers who bump off aging, lonely old men who come to live in their boarding house. On television, there was the program *Dexter*, about a Miami police forensics expert who moonlights as a serial killer; Joe Carroll in *The Following*; a serial killer in *True Detective*; and quite a few serial killers in the series *American Horror Story*. Musicals also have been made about serial killing—Johnny Depp, for example, starred as the demon barber of Fleet Street in the musical *Sweeney Todd*—the story of a barber who kills customers. His accomplice, Mrs. Lovett, bakes the victims into popular meat pies. Viewers may find the stories of serial killers both entertaining and horrifying. Often, serial killers in movies and television are charming, sophisticated, smart, crazy, and evil. They toy with the police, giving clues as to their identity, and seem to want to get caught. While some of these traits may hold true for some real-life serial killers, the truth is that most serial killers are probably not as charming and debonair as those portrayed in fiction.

Often, real-life serial killers seem like ordinary people. As in movies and television shows, they hide their crimes well for a while and appear to the community as upstanding, hardworking citizens: Ted Bundy worked several jobs and pursued a law degree; Jeffrey Dahmer worked a steady job at a chocolate factory; the Bind-Torture-Kill (BTK) killer worked for ADT Security; and the Green River killer had a job painting trucks for thirty years.

The truth behind these seemingly normal lifestyles fascinates us. Actions that are so outside the norm often attract people, Dr. Scott Bonn says in his book *Why We Love Serial Killers*. "People are drawn to understanding the dark side, and the dark side is part of the human condition."[1] Therese Jones, associate director of the Center for Bioethics and Humanities at the University of Colorado in Boulder, says that people may not feel guilt enjoying repulsive behavior because this behavior is unpreventable.[2] For many, the serial killer's actions cannot be comprehended or controlled, and because of this, people feel justified in being absorbed in the topic without feeling bad because there's nothing they can do to change the outcomes.

Whether it's a real serial killer or a fictional one, people also want to know what makes this type of person tick. What motivates him? What makes her kill? Why does he kill in such a gruesome way? People want to make some sense out of something that seems to make no sense whatsoever. Ultimately, that may be why people are fascinated by these killers.

The TV shows and movies that feature serial killers, however, rarely convey the true pain, suffering, and grief that results from these killings. Those who are friends and family of the victims suffer a huge loss and wrenching emotional pain that can last for years or often a lifetime.

From all the media attention given to serial killers, it may seem as if we are all in danger of being victims. Scott Bonn points out that no more than one percent of all murders committed in America are serial killings, based on statistics from the Federal Bureau of Investigation (FBI).[3] Still, that's quite a few serial killings, considering the fact that about fifteen thousand murders are committed annually in this country. (Worldwide, the United Nations Office on Drugs and Crime has reported that 437,000 people were murdered in 2012.)[4] The US numbers would indicate that no more than 150 people are victims of serial killers annually and that no more than twenty-five to fifty serial killers are actively killing at any given time. Even though there are about 320 million people in the United States, it still may not be comforting to know that up to fifty of them are serial killers.[5]

There seemed to be a growing trend in serial killing in the twentieth century. At least four hundred serial killers struck during that century, with 80 percent occurring from the 1950s on. However, *Slate* magazine reported that serial killings appear to be tapering off after an upward trend. In the 1960s, there were nineteen serial killings. The number shot up to 119 in the 1970s and increased further to two hundred in the 1980s. Then in the 1990s, the number of cases dipped to 141. By the 2000s, serial killer cases dropped even lower, to sixty-one.[6]

What Is a Serial Killer?

What defines a serial killer? It may be helpful to first examine what a serial killer is *not*. A serial killer is not a mass murderer—a person who snaps and kills a group of people at one time. Student Seung-Hui Cho shot and killed thirty-two people on Virginia Tech's campus in 2007. James Holmes shot and killed twelve people and injured seventy in a rampage at a Colorado movie theater on July 20, 2012. Anders Behring Breivik killed seventy-seven people near Oslo, Norway, in 2011. Sixty-nine of them were attending a youth camp. These are all examples of mass murderers.

Spree killers murder in multiple locations and within a short period of time. One example of a spree killer is Charles Whitman, an ex-Marine and sniper, who killed his mother and his wife before proceeding to a tower at the University of Texas, where he used his skills as an expert marksman to shoot fourteen people.

Serial killers also do not commit "crimes of passion." Some murder from a sudden strong impulse of anger or heartbreak. They do, however, murder strangers. They take a sick pleasure in killing for killing's sake. They usually work alone.

What about political killings? Democidal killers such as dictators and tyrants who murder many people over time on behalf of their government are not categorized as serial killers. Sometimes the lines can blur, however. If a ruler uses his power to kill just for the thrill of it, he might be deemed a serial killer. One of the earliest of this type of killer was Liu Pengli from the second century BCE, who killed just because he could.

The Types and Behaviors of Serial Killers

	Organized	Disorganized
IQ	105–120 (falls within normal range)	80–95 (below average)
Social skills	Normal	Poor
Childhood	Grew up with a stable father or father figure; may have encountered physical abuse	Grew up with an abusive father or no father present; may have encountered emotional abuse
Proximity of murders to home	Moves around a lot to flee murder scenes	Commits murders around home
Living situation	Married, lives with partner, or dates	Lives alone, doesn't date
Education	Possibly attended college	Dropped out of high school
Time of activity	Daytime	Night-time
Method of ensnaring victims	Seduction	Attack
Interaction with victims	Converses with victims	Does not consider victims to be people
Method of disposal	May dismember body after killing; disposes of remains	Leaves body behind after killing; usually does not dismember
State of crime scene	Controlled; little physical evidence left behind	Chaotic; leaves physical evidence behind
Reason for returning to scene of crime	To see the police working; interest in police work	To re-live the murder

Source: O'Connor, Tom. "Serial Killer Typology."
http://www.ravenndragon.net/montgomery/csi/oconnortypology1.pdf

Historical Serial Killers

The term *serial killer* refers to killing several people over a period of time. Some experts have said it has to be more than three people over the course of a month or more. Some simply define it as the killing of two or more victims in separate events. One edition of the FBI's official *Crime Classification Manual* says that at least three different murder events at three different locations must occur with breaks between these events for the murders to be called serial killings.[7] Some killers have brought victims back to the same location and they have been called serial killers. John Allen Muhammed and Lee Boyd Malvo killed at least ten people in 2002 in a series of murders called the Beltway sniper attacks. They killed people as they pumped gas, sat waiting for the bus, and mowed grass. In 1997, Andrew Cunanan went on a cross-country killing spree, murdering at least five people, including the famous designer Gianni Versace.

The *phrase serial killer* may have been first used by the director of Berlin's criminal police unit, Ernst August Ferdinand Gennat. In the 1930s, he referred to Peter Kürten as a *serienmörder* or in English—a serial killer. Kürten was dubbed the Vampire of Düsseldorf and the Düsseldorf Monster for killing nine women and girls.

The use of the term became more popular when FBI Special Agent Robert Ressler used it in reference to David Berkowitz (also known as "The Son of Sam"), who killed six people in New York City between 1976 and 1977.[8]

TYPES OF SERIAL KILLERS

There are several ways to categorize serial killers based on their mental states, motives, and behaviors. Most experts agree on the following categories:

Psychopathic vs. Psychotic

Psychologists often divide serial killers into two main groups: psychopathic (or organized) and psychotic (or disorganized). Former FBI profiler Roy Hazelwood helped create this structure or approach to better understand serial killers.[1]

The Crime Museum in Washington, DC, explains the two types.[2] The psychopathic or organized killers are often clever and fairly meticulous. They plan carefully and go through great pains to make sure they do not leave behind clues to their identity. They may track potential victims for days, deciding who will be a suitable target. They're often well equipped with tools, locations, and details on how to kill and dispose of a person. They frequently gain the victim's trust—

faking emotions or gaining sympathy—and take great pride in how they are able to kill and get away with it. Typically they seem like normal people. Bonn has said that these killers are true psychopaths—people who suffer from chronic mental disorder and exhibit abnormal or violent social behavior. Sometimes they will take pleasure in stumping law enforcement professionals who are trying to catch them.

Psychotic or disorganized serial killers do not plan ahead at all. Their victims just tend to be in the wrong place at the wrong time. These killers seem to murder just when the moment and circumstances feel right. They usually make no effort to cover up their crimes. They are likely to leave blood, fingerprints, and the murder weapon behind. Their violent acts are often messy. They move around to different locations, towns, and states to avoid capture. They typically have lower intelligence quotients (IQs) than the organized killers. They may feel compelled by visions or voices they hear in their head. They usually have a form of psychosis, an extreme mental disorder in which thoughts and emotions are so impaired that they have lost a grasp on reality. They have an inability to maintain relationships, and they may be abusing drugs or alcohol.

Sometimes the criminals are "mixed offenders" who cannot be easily classified as either psychopathic or psychotic, as organized or disorganized.

Medical Killers

The Crime Museum distinguishes the "medical killer" as a distinct type of serial killer. This person cares for people in a hospital or other medical setting but uses drugs or other means to kill off victims and make it seem as if the death has been natural. Some

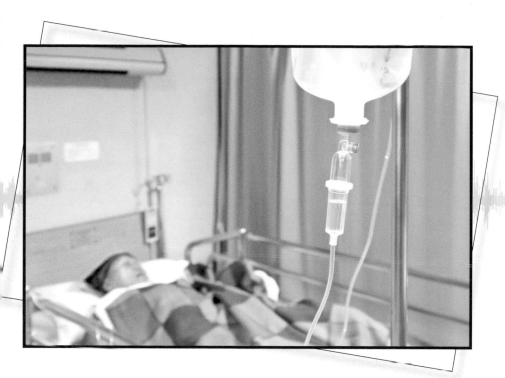

Some medical serial killers prey on people who are vulnerable, such as patients in hospitals. These people may be killing for the thrill of it, to gain money or notoriety, or in the belief they are relieving patients from their suffering.

nurses and doctors have been able to kill many people without others catching on because death is a comon occurrence in hospitals and is easily accepted. Some of these medical killers think they are doing God's work, relieving patients of their suffering on Earth.

Act-focused vs. Process-focused

Ronald M. Holmes and Stephen T. Holmes are authors who have studied serial killers at great length. They have come up with other ways to classify and understand killers and their behaviors.[3] They

Historical Serial Killers

It is highly unlikely that you will fall victim to a serial killer. Films, books, and TV shows make it seem more possible, playing on the pleasure that many people get from feeling afraid.

have distinguished serial killers as act-focused or process-focused. Act-focused murderers kill quickly, while process-focused killers kill slowly and methodically, taking enjoyment from the torture and slow death of their victims.

Within the act-focused category there are "visionary" and "missionary" killers. Visionary serial killers hear voices or see visions that instruct them to kill. The voices are often from God or the Devil. The criminal justifies his acts because he believes he was told by a higher power to commit the heinous deeds. Missionary serial killers feel that they must eliminate a group of people from the earth. This group may be prostitutes, foreigners, or people of a distinct race. Missionary serial killers can often come across as quiet, decent people on the surface.

The process-focused killers may be separated into four categories: gain, lust, thrill, and power. Gain killers are the rarest of serial killers, but their motivations are distinct: They eliminate others for personal or financial gain. In the movie *The Talented Mr. Ripley*, for instance, the title character played by Matt Damon kills to gain and maintain social status and wealth.

Lust killers may be the largest category of serial killers. These criminals get some sort of sexual satisfaction from killing. Also, they are often sadists, who get pleasure from making people suffer. They are organized killers who spend time carefully planning how they will take advantage of someone. They are often thought to go through four phases of behavior. First, they have twisted fantasies about killing and sex, and they may be into pornography. Then, they shift into a reality phase where they hunt a victim. They carefully study the victim and learn about their target's habits and life so when they attack they will have control over the situation. They may track someone for days, weeks, months, even a year or more. In the kill stage, the lust killer will take great care to make sure the victim is secure and in a place that is safely away from possible intruders. Then, when the moment feels right, the killers may go off the deep end and torture, mutilate, or dismember the victim. They may take part in truly revolting behavior, eating part of the victim (cannibalism) or having sex with the dead body (necrophilia). In the postkill phase, the perpetrators might feel depressed and empty inside. They can feel tormented by their own sick behavior and only

The Talented Mr. Ripley (1999) tells the story of Tom Ripley (Matt Damon), a skilled liar and manipulator who stops at nothing to get what he wants. Many psychologists would label Mr. Ripley as a sociopath.

find relief by taking other lives. The killers may reach out to law enforcement or the press indicating that they have killed and may kill again.

Thrill killers are similar to lust killers. They do not get sexual gratification from killing, but taking lives stimulates them and makes them feel pleasure. It can feel like a drug-induced high.

Power killers are similar to lust killers and thrill killers. These criminals feel like they are playing God. Killing makes them feel

Deborah Schurman-Kauflin, PhD, explains some of the psychology behind cannibalism in her article, "Why Cannibals Love Eating People," in *Psychology Today*. She says that cannibals are extreme loners. When they kill and eat a victim, they feel less alone. That person is with them all the time. The victim becomes part of the cannibals. The killing and eating are stimulating and intoxicating and they must do it again. For the cannibals, killing, cutting up, and eating someone stimulates the pleasure center. Each cut may bring pleasure, so the process itself is exciting. They usually go to great lengths to hide their behavior, but they can be very proud of their actions and think it an acceptable practice because they are cannibals and it is simply in their nature to eat other people.[4]

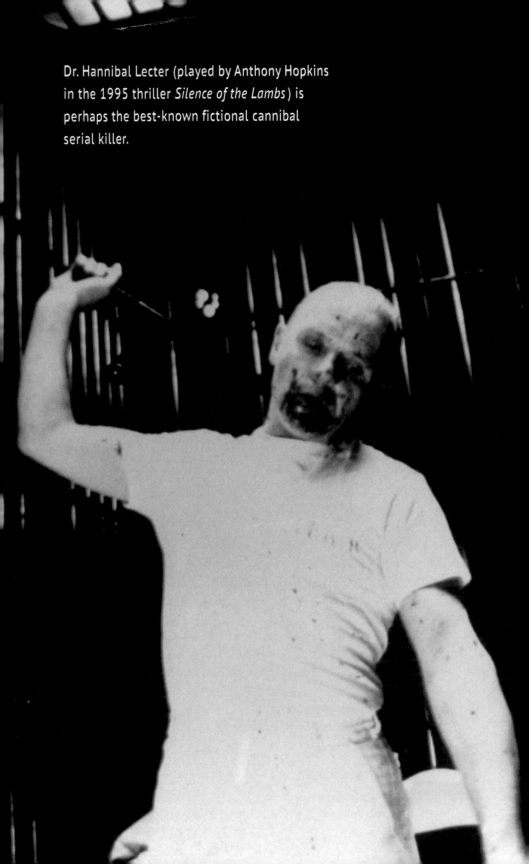

Dr. Hannibal Lecter (played by Anthony Hopkins in the 1995 thriller *Silence of the Lambs*) is perhaps the best-known fictional cannibal serial killer.

they are almighty and cannot be stopped. The fictional character Hannibal Lecter is said to be a power killer.

Stable vs. Transient

The website Serial Killers Defined also defines serial murderers as either "stable" or "transient." Stable killers like to stay put in one area—like Jeffrey Dahmer, the Green River killer, and the BTK killer. They do not travel much, remain in one area, and kill people in their neighborhood where they are comfortable. Transient killers keep on the move, shifting locations, killing as they go. Part of the reason they are on the move is to avoid capture.

Chapter 2

Part of solving and preventing serial killers' crimes is understanding why they do what they do. This is called "criminal profiling." Criminal profiling is the science of creating a psychological sketch of a criminal based on available evidence and witness reports. The infamous Jack the Ripper case is said to be the start of modern criminal profiling. For this case, Dr. Thomas Bond developed a profile based on clues the Ripper left behind. He believed that the murderer was not very remarkable in appearance or manner because he had to gain the trust of victims so he could approach them. He most likely wore a long coat to cover blood spatter, which would allow him to walk away from his crimes without detection. Perhaps he was a surgeon or butcher because he could subdue, kill, and remove the organs from a victim within just fifteen minutes.[1]

Getting to the heart of why serial killers kill begins with a common debate known as Nature vs. Nurture. Some say killers are

Many psychologists posit that a stable home and family life during childhood will dissuade a person with sociopathic or psychopathic tendencies from becoming violent.

born a certain way and can't help themselves. Others say that people become killers as a result of their upbringing.

Nature vs. Nuture

Kira Dawn Wissman writes in an article titled "Nature vs. Nurture: Serial Killers and Social Psychology" that up to 60 percent of what makes a person a serial killer is biological and the remaining 40 percent may be attributed to environmental factors.[2]

Historical Serial Killers

Some people say that serial killers are wired differently from others from birth. They may be born self-centered, impulsive, and driven by anger. Jim Fallon, a neuroscientist and professor at the University of California, has been studying the brains of psychopathic killers. In a TED Talk that he gave in July 2009, Fallon said that he has studied many brains and the ones belonging to murderers and serial killers all had "damage to their orbital cortex, which is right above the eyes, the orbits, and also the interior part of the temporal lobe." They may have been born with the damage or it may have come later.[3]

The psychologist Sigmund Freud studied human behavior extensively. According to Freud's theory of personality development, a child's behavior is shaped mostly by the interactions that he has with the world before he is five years old.[4] The way an infant is treated is crucial to his or her development. If a child does not have adequate touch, love, and support as a child, he or she can develop a personality disorder. Many serial killers have suffered some sort of child abuse. Many were in difficult family situations or had absent fathers. Some studies claim that 16 percent of serial killers were adopted. An article from Le Moyne College titled "The Psychology of a Serial Killer" presents these statistics about convicted serial killers:

- **42** percent suffered from physical abuse as children
- **74** percent suffered from psychological abuse
- **35** percent witnessed sexual abuse
- **43** percent were sexually abused themselves
- **29** percent were found to be accident-prone children[5]

"Nature vs. nurture" is a theory strongly debated among psychologists. Many psychologists believe that the cycle of abuse is likely to continue if a person is mistreated as a child.

Serial killer Jeffrey Dahmer was said to have a happy childhood until about age six, when hernia surgery, a move to a new town, and the birth of a younger brother seemed to change him. His insecurities and shyness grew. Still, many people move to a new town without becoming serial killers. Perhaps the explanation for him becoming a killer was both in his nature and the events that shaped his life.

The MacDonald Triad

From years of studying killers and other sociopaths (people with mental disorders that make them very antisocial and who lack any conscience), psychologists and psychiatrists have discovered

Arson is one of three indicators that a person might have homicidal tendencies.

certain common behaviors that may suggest a person might become homicidal later. The big three indicators have been dubbed the MacDonald Triad, named after the psychiatrist J. M. MacDonald, who first proposed them.[6] The characteristics are bed-wetting, arson, and cruelty to animals. MacDonald found that these behaviors could later lead to homicidal tendencies and possibly sexually predatory behavior. These behaviors may occur because of childhood neglect, abuse, or brutality.

Reaching back in history, we often don't have clues to the profiles or motivations of serial killers. Still, it is fascinating to know that serial killing is not a modern phenomenon.

Chapter 3

PROFILES OF SERIAL KILLERS THROUGHOUT HISTORY

Almost as long as mankind has lived on planet Earth, there have been sick individuals who take pleasure from killing others. Back in the days of Roman emperors and monarchs, many rulers had their enemies killed. What defines a serial killer may be a bit blurry in early history. Also, note that many serial killers prior to the 1900s were women who often poisoned their victims. There are certainly still women serial killers in the modern world, but the pages of history reveal a surprising number of dastardly females.

Locusta of Gaul

Born: **First century AD**

Location: **Ancient Rome, born in Gaul, now France**

Profession: **Herbalist/botanist**

Motive: **Gain**

Date of capture: **October 68 AD**

Date of death: **68 AD**

Locusta of Gaul holds claim to fame for being one of the first recorded serial killers in history. Growing up in the countryside, she learned the properties of many plants. She knew which ones could heal and which ones could cause harm. When she became an adult, she traveled to the big city of Rome. Here she learned that people were greedy and that many would do almost anything to build their wealth—including killing people they knew. However, those who wanted to inherit fortunes from their relatives couldn't simply kill them.

Murder was (in general) regarded as a serious crime, but Locusta had the means of poisoning people with natural ingredients so it would appear that they died of natural causes. She tested her deadly recipes on animals, reportedly using hemlock, nightshade, arsenic, quinine, and possibly even cyanide and opium. Soon, she was very much in demand for her services and people in Rome were suddenly

In this illustration, Roman Emperor Nero (AD 39–68) watches as Locusta tries out a poison on a helpless slave. Locusta was the first recorded serial killer. The emperor agreed to pardon Locusta for her crimes if she would assassinate his enemies for him.

dropping like flies. She was arrested several times under suspicion of poisoning but had many powerful clients who saw to her release.

In the year 54 AD, the Empress Agrippina called upon Locusta. As the fourth wife of the Roman Emperor Claudius, Agrippina was the most powerful woman in the land. She had a beloved son, Nero, from a former marriage. She wanted Nero to be emperor and she would do all in her power to make it so. The sixty-four-year-old emperor enjoyed eating mushrooms, and as the story goes, Agrippina thought that using poisoned mushrooms to dispose of her husband would disguise the crime perfectly. Although not 100 percent verified, one story says that Locusta poisoned the mushrooms, which Agrippina herself served to her husband. Agrippina feigned horror as her husband doubled over with stomach cramps. By October 13, 54 AD, Claudius was dead and young Nero was now the ruler of the Roman Empire.

Locusta was eventually accused of poisoning Claudius and was arrested. Nero, however, found a way to have her released—he wanted to use her services again. Claudius had a fourteen-year-old son from a previous marriage named Britannicus. Nero saw the young boy as a threat to the throne so he found a clever way to have

In this painting, Emperor Nero watches as his mother dies.

the young man's wine poisoned at a dinner party. Britannicus had epilepsy. When he began to convulse on the floor before a group of guests, Nero told them not to worry, saying it was Britannicus's epilepsy. The young man died a few hours later.

Nero was delighted with the results and gave Locusta a full pardon. She grew wealthier and was well respected (and feared). Nero gave her a grand villa. She was hired by many for her special contract work. She even opened a school to pass on to others her expertise in herbs, plants, and their toxic properties. Nero eventually grew tired of his mother's interference and even had Agrippina put to death. He had many rivals killed and lapsed into hedonistic and tyrannical ways. Eventually, the Roman Senate condemned Nero to death. He decided to kill himself in 68 AD. Without her protector, Locusta was arrested and put to death in that same year.[1]

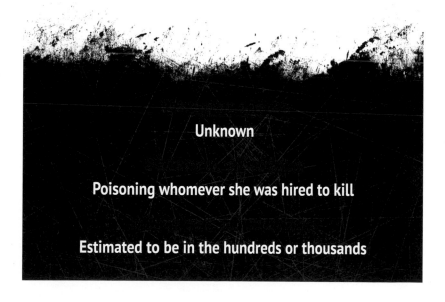

Unknown

Poisoning whomever she was hired to kill

Estimated to be in the hundreds or thousands

Gilles de Rais

Born: **September 10, 1404**
Location: **France**
Profession: **French noble**
Motive: **Lust or thrill**
Date of capture: **October 1440**
Date of death: **October 26, 1440**

Gilles de Rais is among the earliest serial killers. He had a sadistic and psychopathic nature. As a young man de Rais had a distinguished career and was known to be very ambitious. In the 1420s, he fought in wars against the English. He gained a position as a guard for Joan of Arc and fought by her side in many battles, waged to reclaim France from England in the Hundred Years War. The visionary seventeen-year-old peasant girl Joan of Arc inspired the French army and led them to many victories against the English, including a crucial battle at Orleans in 1429.

King Charles VII made de Rais a marshall of France. He continued to serve as Joan of Arc's guard, up until she was captured by the English in 1430. (She burned at the stake in 1431 at the age of nineteen for her crimes against the English. She became officially canonized in 1920. She was known as the Maid of Orléans and has become one of history's greatest saints and an enduring symbol of French unity and nationalism.)[2]

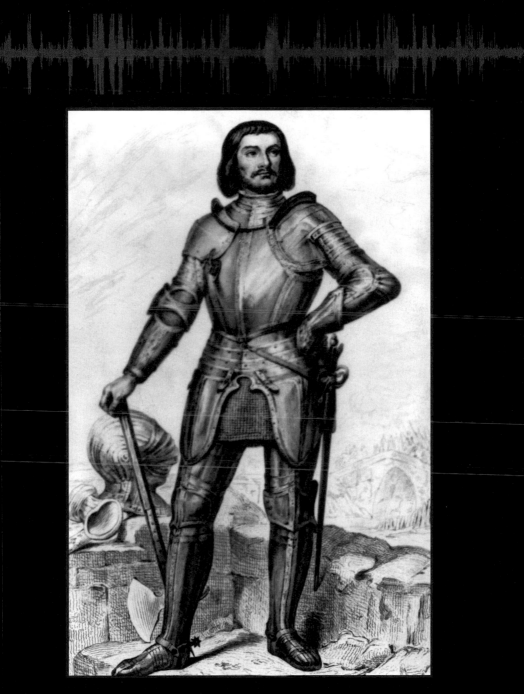

It is possible that Gilles de Rais developed a taste for killing during his service in the Hundred Years War.

After Joan of Arc was captured, de Rais retired as a baron, knight, and lord. He had inherited enormous amounts of land and married a wealthy heiress, and he might have earned an honorable place in French history, but his path took a dark turn at this point. He squandered his riches, keeping a large chateau with a huge staff of servants and putting on lavish theatrical pageants.

Fearing complete financial ruin, de Rais's family prevented him from selling any more of his land, at which point he turned to the occult. De Rais met a sorcerer named Francesco Prelati, who reportedly could speak to demons and change metals into gold. Prelati convinced de Rais that he could regain his dwindling wealth by turning to Satanism and sacrificing children to a demon. He captured unaccompanied children in the nearby village and countryside. It was said that de Rais took sexual pleasure in watching children die. He would rape, torture, and mutilate them. Sometimes he would cut off their heads. Sometimes he would sit on their chests as they were dying. Other times he would throw them out the window. He supposedly had a penchant for children who were blonde haired and blue eyed.

Despite his brutal actions, de Rais maintained a strong connection with the Catholic Church. In May 1440, de Rais had a disagreement with clergyman Jean le Ferron at the Church of Saint Etienne de Mer Morte. The clergyman was kidnapped and de Rais was the primary suspect. The ensuing investigation led to the discovery of de Rais's horrific crimes. He was accused of abducting, torturing, and murdering more than 140 children. Transcripts from witnesses were so repulsive they were stricken from the records.

Gilles de Rais initially denied the charges, but ultimately confessed under threat of torture and excommunication. He was

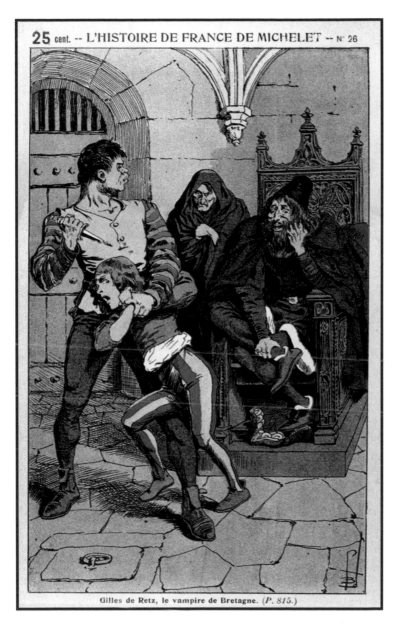

25 cent. -- L'HISTOIRE DE FRANCE DE MICHELET -- N° 26

Gilles de Retz, le vampire de Bretagne. (*P. 815.*)

Following the guidance of a diabolical advisor, Gilles de Rais tried to regain his wealth by torturing and killing young children.

Gilles de Rais was convicted of murder and sentenced to death by hanging and burning. On October 26, 1440, he was hanged and a fire was lit at his feet. However, he was judged to be penitent and his body was cut down before it was consumed by the fire.

condemned for heresy by the church and convicted of murder by the courts. Sentenced to death by hanging and burning, he was hanged on October 26, 1440. Because he repented for his crimes, de Rais's body was removed from the gallows before it burned.[3,4]

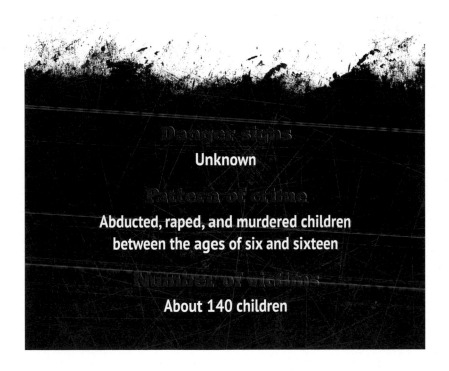

Danger signs

Unknown

Pattern of crime

Abducted, raped, and murdered children between the ages of six and sixteen

Number of victims

About 140 children

Liu Pengli

Born: **Second century BC, date unknown**
Location: **Jidong, China**
Profession: **King**
Motive: **Thrill**
Date of capture: **144 BC**
Date of death: **Second century BC, date unknown**

Liu Pengli is one of the earliest-known serial killers in recorded history. Cousin to Emperor Jing of the Han dynasty in China, he served as the ruler of the city of Jidong for about twenty-three years, from 144 to 121 BCE. In the ancient Chinese text known as the *Records of the Grand Historian*, Pengli is said to have murdered at least a hundred people and seized their belongings for sport. He regularly hunted common people with groups of slaves or young men hiding from capture by the law. He murdered many of those people and took others as slaves. His horrific deeds were well known throughout the land and many citizens were afraid to leave their homes at night. Eventually, a son of one of the victims told the emperor of China about Pengli's crimes.

風俗移易人民富庶
蕩薄彝倫常永終譽

漢景帝

Liu Pengli was spared the death penalty because his cousin, Emperor Jing of Han (depicted here), did not want to kill a relative.

The court of the land found him guilty and recommended that he be executed for his crimes. The emperor, however, could not bring himself to kill his relative, so Pengli was stripped of his royal title, exiled, and never heard from again.[5]

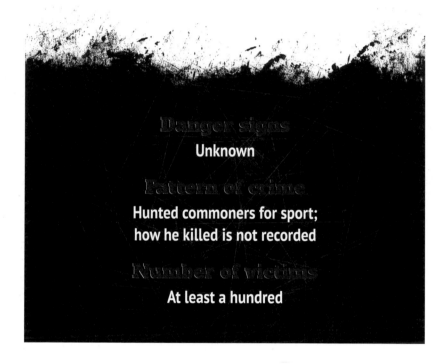

Danger signs
Unknown

Pattern of crime
Hunted commoners for sport; how he killed is not recorded

Number of victims
At least a hundred

Peter Stumpp

aka Peter Stubbe or Stumf and
"The Werewolf of Bedburg"

Born: Unknown

Location: Bedburg in Western Germany's Rhineland

Profession: Farmer

Motive: Thrill

Date of capture: 1589

Date of death: October 31, 1589

Peter Stumpp was a respected and wealthy farmer near Cologne, Germany. He was known throughout the region as a genial man. Some say his real name wasn't Stumpp and that he got the name when his left hand was accidentally cut off—all that remained was a stump. Stumpp had a family, but his wife died and left him to care for their son and daughter alone.

Religious conflict was erupting between Catholics and Protestants in the Rhine region. The Black Death added to their troubles, taking many lives. At the same time, local farmers became puzzled and anxious about a growing number of deaths among their cattle. These keepers of livestock were finding cows brutally slaughtered in their fields. The hides were torn open and their guts were often strewn on the ground. Goats and sheep were also savagely killed. The townspeople were puzzled by what creature could cause the gruesome mutilations.

The problem grew more serious when children and young women started to disappear. A few were discovered torn apart like the cattle. Some people speculated that wolves were to blame, while others thought that it was the work of a werewolf. No one suspected the kindly farmer Stumpp—at least not at first. Some reports said that Stumpp was attracted to the dark side, even when he was a child. At age twelve, he was said to have an interest in magic, witchcraft, and necromancy (communicating with the dead).

At his trial, Stumpp said that the Devil himself gave him a gift when he was twelve—it was wolf's fur. Stumpp said that the fur transformed him and allowed him to carry out evil deeds. It gave him "the likeness of a greedy, devouring wolf, strong and mighty, with eyes great and large, which in the night sparkled like brands of fire; a mouth great and wide, with most sharp and cruel teeth; a huge body and mighty paws."

Dressed as a wolf, he beat and strangled thirteen children and then tore them to pieces. He'd rip their throats open, disembowel them, and eat parts of them. He murdered two pregnant women and then forcibly pulled out the fetuses from their wombs and "ate their hearts panting hot and raw." He called the fetuses "dainty morsels."

Stumpp supposedly loved his own children. He called his son the light of his life, but his dark yearnings eventually turned him to attack his own children. He had an incestuous relationship with his daughter, and he killed his son and ate his brain.

For a while, the townspeople could not find the monster who was murdering their women and children. Stumpp would dress

Peter Stumpp was called "the Werewolf of Bedburg" because of his preferred method of killing. This reproduction of a 16th-century woodcut tells the story of "Stubbe Peter the Werewolf."

Peter Stumpp was brutally tortured to death in public in 1589 to discourage others from committing equally brutal crimes.

elegantly and walk among the townspeople, greeting them as if he were totally guiltless. For about twenty-five years, Stumpp carried out his crimes until one day a group of townspeople formed a hunting team and cornered the "wolf" one night. When they caught the beast, they saw it was Stumpp dressed in his wolf skin.

After he was caught, tried, and tortured, he confessed to the crimes. His punishment was the following: "Peter Stubbe is sentenced to be broken by a wheel and to tearing of his flesh in ten different places by hot pincers so that it is separated from the bone, then to the quartering of legs and arms by wooden sticks or hammers, next to beheading and finally burning to ash." The wheel upon which Stumpp was broken was hung on a pole and displayed in the town to discourage others from such activities. Above the wheel people hung a framed likeness of a wolf, and Peter Stumpp's severed head was placed on the pole's sharp point. Some have cast doubts on the story saying that Stumpp may have been a Protestant and therefore targeted during the religious wars of the time. His punishment might have been designed to drive people back to the Catholic religion or "true" church. They also point out that Stumpp confessed under the duress of torture, which is an unreliable method of gaining truthful information.[6,7]

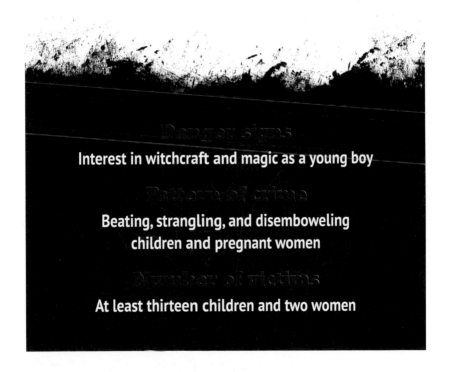

Danger signs

Interest in witchcraft and magic as a young boy

Patterns of crime

**Beating, strangling, and disemboweling
children and pregnant women**

Number of victims

At least thirteen children and two women

Peter Niers
aka Peter Niersch

Born: **1566**

Location: **Neumarkt, Germany**

Profession: **Bandit**

Motive: **Gain**

Date of capture: **September 1581**

Date of death: **September 16, 1581**

At first glance, Peter Niers appears to be just a ruthless robber. He would sometimes work together with other robbers to gain riches. Niers apparently was particularly ruthless and was eventually found guilty of killing 544 people. His victims included twenty-four pregnant women and their fetuses.

By some accounts, Niers needed fetuses to practice the black arts and do the work of the Devil. To cast spells, he may have eaten fetus hearts. There were stories of thieves like Niers making candles from infant flesh. They used the candles to see when they robbed homes. Various rumors told tales of Niers turning invisible or changing into an animal or even into a log or stone. By some accounts, he was a master of disguise, eluding capture by posing as a beggar or soldier.

One story of his arrest said he checked into an inn and then proceeded on to a local bathhouse. For safekeeping, he left his bag of magical ingredients in the care of the innkeeper. This bag aroused suspicion. People suspected that he may be the notorious killer. Local police asked the innkeeper if they could look in his bag while he was out. They are said to have found several cut-off hands and hearts from murdered fetuses.

Niers's execution was recorded in more detail than any of the abhorrent crimes he committed. Because he was such a brutal killer, the justice system condemned him to a brutal death as well. But first he was tortured alive. Using hot oils, his flesh was stripped from his body. Over three days, he was attached to and broken by a torture device called the Wheel. His death finally came while being quartered (chopped into four pieces or pulled apart by attaching a rope to the limbs and then to four different horses, which then ran outward in different directions). Because Niers confessed under torture, some are not fully convinced of his guilt.[8,9]

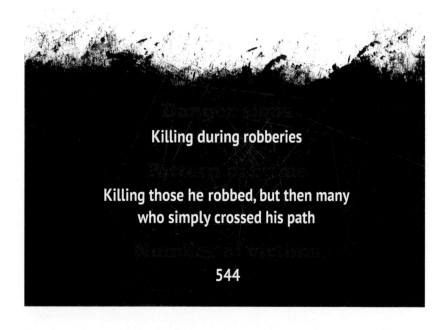

Killing during robberies

Killing those he robbed, but then many who simply crossed his path

544

Gilles Garnier
aka "The Werewolf of Dole" and "The Hermit of St. Bonnot"

Born: **1500s**

Location: **Dole, France**

Profession: **Hermit**

Motive: **Thrill or gain**

Date of capture: **December 1573**

Date of death: **January 8, 1574**

The 1500s was a time of global exploration and great literature from Shakespeare, but it was also a time of religious turmoil and religious wars. While Germany had its "werewolf" Peter Stumpp, France had its own gory man-beast in Gilles Garnier. Garnier was known to be a quiet hermit his whole life, living in the Franche-Comte province. The isolated Garnier met and married a woman, and villagers described the couple as sullen recluses.

As the story goes, Garnier was able to barely provide for himself while he lived alone, but when his wife came along he ran into difficulty. A short while after his marriage in 1573, local children began to disappear. Their mutilated bodies would later be discovered. The first reported attack came in November of that year. Peasants who were walking home from work through the woods heard the cries of a young girl. When they ran to help her, they saw the child defending herself from what looked like a large wolf. Seeing the people approach, the creature ran off on what appeared to be all fours. The girl was seriously wounded but survived. Some said it must be a werewolf. Others thought it could possibly be the hermit.

In the weeks to come, one boy disappeared and two girls and another boy were found slain. A couple of adults were attacked but survived. Rumors spread about a werewolf, and on December 3, 1573, the government issued a decree to hunt the werewolf. Shortly thereafter, a group of men who were hunting the beast spied the wolf hunched over a child's body. As they approached, they recognized that it was the hermit.

Garnier told the authorities the lurid accounts of his killings. He grabbed one little twelve-year-old girl and dragged her into a vineyard. There, he murdered the child by tearing her apart with his teeth and hands. He acted like a wolf, pulling her bleeding body along the ground with his teeth into the nearby wood. Once hidden out of sight in the woods, he ate most of her at one meal and then brought the leftovers home for his wife to enjoy. He was said to have killed a thirteen-year-old boy in a similar fashion. He ate part of him and gnawed off an arm and leg, which he hid in the woods to eat later.

Fifty witnesses testified against him, but he also confessed when he was put on the rack. He was found guilty of killing two girls and two boys, as well as practicing witchcraft and lycanthropy (the supernatural transformation of a person into a wolf). He was condemned and, on January 18, 1573, burned alive at the stake. The court had also ordered him to pay for the cost of his prosecution.[10]

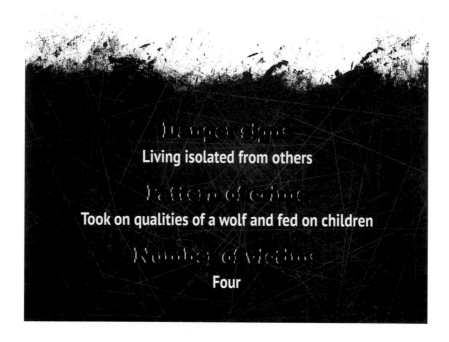

Danger signs
Living isolated from others

Pattern of crime
Took on qualities of a wolf and fed on children

Number of victims
Four

Elizabeth Báthory
aka *"The Blood Countess"*

Born: **August 7, 1560**

Location: **Hungary**

Profession: **Countess**

Motive: **Thrill**

Date of capture: **December 1610**

Date of death: **August 21, 1614**

Sometimes described as the most vicious, sadistic serial killer in history, Elizabeth Báthory grew up in a life of privilege. She not only had good looks, she also had great wealth and an excellent education. However, some of her family members were seriously disturbed, and they may have shaped her later life. An uncle taught her about Satanism, and an aunt instructed her in sadomasochism.

By the age of eleven or twelve, Báthory was engaged to be married to Ferenc Nadasdy, who was from another aristocratic family. Before the wedding, Báthory had a baby with another man. When Nadasdy learned of this, he had that man castrated and attacked by a pack of dogs. The baby was hidden.

After the wedding, the couple made their home in Cachtice Castle and had four children. However, Nadasdy soon discovered his wife had an insatiable appetite for inflicting pain on others, and

The Blood Countess was accused of torturing and murdering hundreds of servant girls.

he would do anything to please his love, including building a torture chamber at her request. Báthory went on to torture servant girls by jamming pins and needles under their fingernails. She beat, stabbed, mutilated, and burned them with hot metal irons. Some girls were chained up at night and shackled until their hands turned blue. Báthory tied down others, covered them in honey, and then left them to be attacked by insects. She was endlessly creative in finding ways to torture people, and her behavior worsened when her husband died in the early 1600s.

Peasant girls were captured, brought to the castle, and never left. Girls from well-to-do families who were sent to Báthory to learn proper aristocratic behavior disappeared at the castle. And, according to some reports, Báthory acquired a taste for drinking human blood because she thought it would keep her looking healthy and young. She was believed to have bitten off the flesh of some of her victims and, in one case, to have forced a young girl to cook and eat her own flesh.

As the number of victims grew and daughters of local nobels began to disappear, stories of her ghastly deeds reached Hungary's King Matthias. In January of 1611, Báthory and four of her accomplices were put on trial. They were convicted on a score of charges. Three of her helpers were sentenced to death and one to life imprisonment. Báthory herself escaped execution because of her family's prominence, but she was sentenced to solitary confinement in a tiny room with no windows. She was passed food through small slits in the wall. She was found dead in her room three years later, at the age of fifty-four. [11,12,13]

Taking pleasure in punishing servants

Tortured and killed young women

Estimates of eighty to 650 people

Cachtice Castle was renovated and reopened for tourists in 2014. There visitors can see the room where Báthory was imprisoned and died.

Catalina de los Ríos y Lisperguer

aka "La Quintrala" or
"The Chilean She-Devil"

Born: **1604, date unknown**

Location: **Chile**

Profession: **Landowner**

Motive: **Lust**

Date of capture: **1660**

Date of death: **1665**

Born into a wealthy, landowning family with a German, Spanish, and American Indian background, Catalina de los Ríos y Lisperguer had bright red hair, for which she was famous within her community. Her flaming locks became her signature and she gained the nickname La Quintrala, a name that comes from a red mistletoe found in Patagonia in Argentina.

At this time in Chile's history, the country had been colonized by the Spanish, who spread the Catholic religion throughout the land. Although Catalina's family was very religious, she was lustful and cruel. Because her family owned vast tracts of land, they needed slaves to maintain their properties and farms. Some of the workers were *inquilinos*, laborers who were allowed to live on a landowner's property but had to work without pay for the landowner. La Quintrala is said to have been hedonistic and sexual with a crazed thirst to inflict cruelty on others. She took pleasure in whipping her slaves, and she tortured many to death. The bodies of *inquilinos* piled up on her properties. She was considered a prime example of colonial abuse and oppression.

Occasionally, La Quintrala was brought into the courts and charged with murder. Her family, however, had great influence in the area. She was usually fined, but most charges against her were dismissed. She expanded her murderous ways beyond slaves, going on to kill her own father by feeding him a poisoned chicken. She also tried to have a local priest assassinated, and she tortured one of her lovers to death.

In 1626, she married a wealthy and well-respected nobleman who was twenty years her elder. Married life did nothing to squelch her cruel tendencies. Finally, in 1660 she was put on trial, but the court system moved so slowly that she passed away before judgment could be handed down.

In an odd twist, she became more religious and contributed to the Catholic Church toward the end of her life. The trigger for her renewed faith was a large crucifix that hung in her home. La Quintrala thought that the figure of Jesus was continually admiring her cleavage, so in a fit of rage one day she hurled the large crucifix out the window. It broke into pieces on the ground below. Townspeople reconstructed it and hung it in a local church. The incident moved La Quintrala, and she began to donate generously to the church. On her deathbed, she requested that twenty thousand masses be said for her.[14,15]

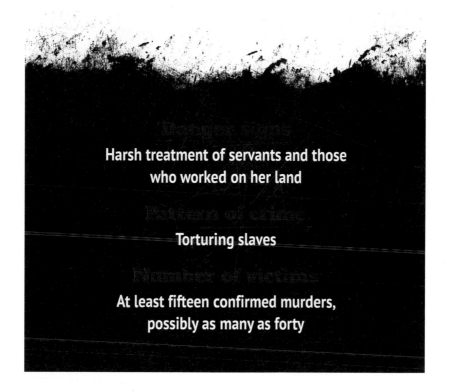

Danger signs

Harsh treatment of servants and those
who worked on her land

Pattern of crime

Torturing slaves

Number of victims

At least fifteen confirmed murders,
possibly as many as forty

Giulia Tofana and Hyeronima Spara

Born: around 1630

Location: Rome and Palermo, Italy

Profession: Potion makers, poisoners, and witches

Motive: Gain

Date of capture: 1659

Date of death: July 1659

For women in the 1600s, life wasn't easy. Considered the property of men, they were powerless to get out of troubled or dangerous marriages and had few places to turn for help. Giulia Tofana and Hyeronima Spara were sympathetic to these women and offered poisons for women who wanted to discreetly free themselves of an oppressive spouse. Murder could solve their problems, and undetectable poison would clear them of suspicion.

Tofana developed a special elixir that eventually won her great renown. Called *Aqua Tofana* (also known as Acqua Toffana), the mixture contained arsenic, lead, and belladonna (a poisonous plant also known as deadly nightshade). The poison was flavorless, colorless, odorless, and impossible to detect after a person died.

Tofana provided her customers with simple instructions to administer the deadly potion in four small doses. The first drop weakened a man and caused symptoms that were similar to those of a cold. With the second dose, his health declined further. The third dose gave the victim's health a serious turn for the worse, and the final dose killed him. So that wives could easily hide the poison among their lotions and perfumes, Tofana sold the elixir concealed in powdered makeup or in vials with the image of St. Nicholas of Bari on them.

Tofana may have been connected to Hyeronima Spara, another poisoner who also considered herself to be a witch. Spara taught the art of poisoning to groups of young women who wanted to become wealthy widows. Tofana and Spara marketed their poisons as a solution for getting rid of abusive, oppressive, or unwanted husbands. The number of publicly weeping but privately grateful widows in Italy began to grow, and sales of their potion were brisk.

According to one story, the professional poisoners were reported by a guilt-ridden wife, who broke down after feeding her husband a bowl of soup spiked with the Aqua Tofana. The would-be murderer told her husband the details of the plan to poison him. The authorities were notified, and they set out to track down and arrest the pair. Tofana had become so popular with the local people that they protected her for a period of time. Ultimately, however, Tofana and Spara were arrested, put on trial, and found to have killed about six hundred men. In July of 1659, they were executed. Some of the women who had purchased the poison and used it were also punished and either imprisoned or themselves killed.[16,17]

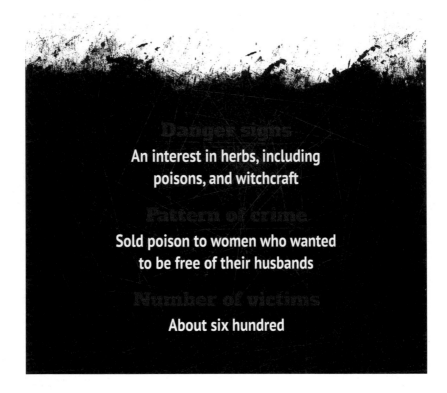

Danger signs

An interest in herbs, including poisons, and witchcraft

Pattern of crime

Sold poison to women who wanted to be free of their husbands

Number of victims

About six hundred

Catherine Monvoisin
aka "La Voisin"

Born: 1640

Location: Paris, France

Profession: Jeweler's wife, fortune-teller, herbalist

Motive: Gain

Date of capture: March 12, 1679

Date of death: February 22, 1680

Catherine Deshayes began her life inauspiciously. She was a homeless street urchin as a young girl. At age nine, she learned the art of fortune-telling. Many of her predictions happened to come true, so she gained a favorable reputation. Many thought she had a gift from God. She was able to earn enough money to lift herself out of poverty.

At age twenty, Catherine married a jeweler, Antoine Monvoisin. When Antoine's business went bust, she returned to fortune-telling. She practiced chiromancy, or palmistry, which is the art of predicting a person's future by reading the lines on the palms of his or her hands. She also foretold the future by reading a customer's face. People who wanted to fall in love came to her to buy amulets and love potions that would help them win hearts. Her ingredients for love powders included bones of toads, the teeth of moles, cantharides (also known as Spanish fly, a type of emerald-green beetle), iron filings, human blood, and human dust.

La Voisin was one of the major figures in the Affair of the Poisons, in which thirty-six members of the elite aristocracy were put to death.

Eventually, people came to La Voisin when they wanted someone in their life to die. So along with aphrodisiacs, she began to sell poisons. The great ladies of Paris apparently flocked to her to partake in many of her services, and the former beggar girl became very wealthy. Some women ordered love potions, and others wanted to murder their husbands' mistresses, but all of these women were among the Parisian elite. La Voisin's poisoning services seemed to be an acceptable practice. *The Rise of Satanism in the Middle Ages* states that she often would meet clients in a darkened chamber wearing an "ermine-lined robe emblazoned with two hundred eagles embroidered in gold thread on purple velvet."

Eventually La Voisin expanded her services to include holding black masses in the subterranean reaches of her house in Paris. These Satanic ceremonies were conducted for people who thought they could get whatever it was they wanted in life by worshipping the devil in this manner. For these masses, La Voisin sacrificed children. Even corrupt Catholic priests attended. One priest who had several mistresses gave up his illegitimate children for the sacrificial killings on the altar.

To get more children, La Voisin opened a home for unwed mothers. She gave these women all the care they needed up until the delivery of the child. After the births, she kept their unwanted children at no charge. In a horrific mockery of a religious mass, a supplicant would lie naked on the altar. The "priest" conducted the ceremony with a prayer book bound in human skin, a chalice of holy urine instead of water, and a toad or a turnip to use as the "host."

These ceremonies cost clients dearly and La Voisin grew even wealthier. She kept these murderous rituals a secret from the police, but eventually a detective named Desgrez discovered her dark rituals. At this time, under the reign of King Louis XIV, there was a certain accepted lack of morals among the elite and well-to-do. Many noble aquaintances of the king were involved in the satanic rituals, including his mistress. Still, he agreed something must be done and La Voisin was arrested. Many in the king's inner circle were protected, but others involved in the dark magic of La Voisin were banished, flogged, or imprisoned. Some accounts say that La Voisin was tortured in four six-hour sessions. At her trial, she boasted that she had slit the throats of more than twenty-five hundred babies. She was burned alive at the stake on the Place de Grève in Paris at the end of February in 1680. As she was led to the stake, she is said to have sung offensive songs and cursed the priests who sought her confession.[18,19]

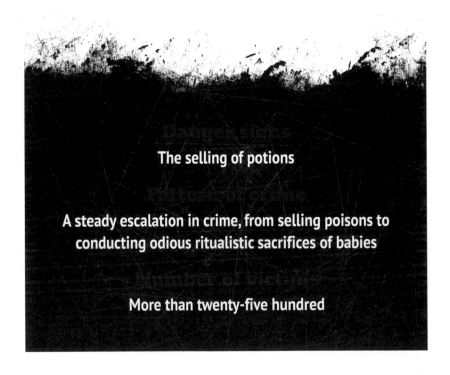

The selling of potions

A steady escalation in crime, from selling poisons to conducting odious ritualistic sacrifices of babies

More than twenty-five hundred

Darya Nikolayevna Saltykova
aka "Saltichikha"

Born: November 3, 1730

Location: Moscow, Russia

Profession: Countess

Motive: Thrill and sadism

Date of capture: May 17, 1764

Date of death: December 27, 1801

Darya Nikolayevna Saltykova gives Elizabeth Báthory a run for her money. The world of nobility seems to have produced a handful of insane sadists. Born as an Ivanova, Darya was married young to Gleb Saltykov, who was from a well-respected and wealthy family. Some described her during her married days as gloomy or unremarkable. She appeared to be devout, contributing a lot to churches and monasteries. When she was twenty-six, her husband died and she became one of the richest widows in all of Moscow. With her two sons, she settled in a large and lavish estate near Moscow called Troitskoe.

She was lonely until she met the young and handsome Nikolay Tyutchev. They began a love affair that lasted for a short time until Darya found out that Tyutchev had met another woman and secretly married her. She went into a rage and almost killed Tyutchev. She wanted both him and his lover dead, but they fled the region before she could act. She turned her rage against her servants, mostly young women. Seeing them all as her rivals, she tortured them—breaking their bones, throwing them out of the house naked into the frost, and pouring boiling water on their bodies. She beat and whipped many to death, including children and pregnant women.

Families began to file complaints with the local magistrates, but initially their pleas for justice fell on deaf ears. The courts respected Darya as a prominent and wealthy woman. They were reluctant to press charges. In time, however, the stories of her cruelties mounted and the authorities had to do something. Her arrest came when one serf escaped and made it to St. Petersburg, the Russian seat of government. The serf filed a petition before the Empress Catherine. The empress wanted to show that she would not stand for such lawless behavior, and she tried Darya publicly.

Darya was arrested on May 17, 1764, and was held for many years as the government conducted its investigation. Many surviving victims and witnesses testified about her dastardly deeds. Darya was visited by a priest during her confinement, but she would not repent. She believed she would be released and could continue as before. But detectives gathered evidence that showed she was guilty of at least 138 murders. Russia had abolished the death penalty in 1754, so on October 2, 1768, Darya was sentenced to life in prison. She was put into complete darkness in a monastery dungeon. Nuns would deliver her food with a candle. When she finished eating, the candle would be taken away. After eleven years, she was transferred to a shuttered room with some light. All in all, she spent thirty-three years imprisoned before she died of natural causes.[20]

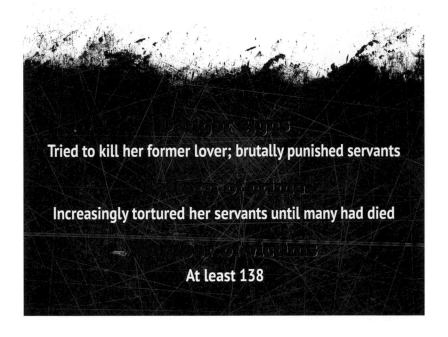

Tried to kill her former lover; brutally punished servants

Increasingly tortured her servants until many had died

At least 138

Lewis Hutchinson
aka "The Mad Master" and
"The Mad Doctor of Edinburgh Castle"

Born: **1733**

Location: **Jamaica**

Profession: **Doctor**

Motive: **Thrill**

Date of capture: **Unknown**

Date of death: **March 16, 1773**

Lewis Hutchinson was a medical doctor who immigrated from Scotland to Jamaica in the 1760s. He came to take care of and gained rights to an estate called Edinburgh Castle. The castle was built by a Scottish architect, who named it after the capital of his mother country. Hutchinson acquired cattle that he raised on the land. Apparently, he acquired them by stealing strays from other nearby farms.

Hutchinson was known to be a keen shot, and he decided that anyone who came near his property was fair game. He would take his rifle and shoot any wayward traveler who came into view. He didn't care who the person was—if he or she was within firing range, he or she was dead. It is said that he killed just for the sport of it. According to some sources, he would feed on the blood of his victims and

Pieces of Edinburgh Castle still stand in Jamaica today. It is thought to be haunted—perhaps by the evil Lewis Hutchinson or maybe by his dozens of victims.

often dismember them. One account said that he took joy in cutting off heads from a "palpitating body" and "the gloomy temper of his soul was sated only by a copious flow of blood." He'd take their bodies and toss them into a sinkhole where animals could feast on the remains. That location became known as Hutchinson's Hole. Later, perhaps out of boredom, he invited guests into his home where he would entertain them first before killing them.

Stories of his murderous ways kept the locals living in fear, and few wanted to venture to his property to confront him. John Callendar, a young English soldier, bravely volunteered to bring in Hutchinson. But the Mad Doctor shot and killed the young man. The uproar was so great after this that the government immediately issued a warrant for his arrest. Aware that Callendar's fellow soldiers would now be after him, Hutchinson fled. He tried to escape by sea but Admiral Rodney and the Royal Navy captured him.

Hutchinson pleaded not guilty, but the evidence showed otherwise. Investigators found forty-three watches, clothing, and other items that proved his guilt. Testimony from his slaves confirmed that he had committed horrendous acts. A court found Hutchinson guilty of the murder of John Callendar, and he was hanged in Spanish Town on March 16, 1773. He had his tombstone inscribed: "Their sentence, pride and malice, I defy; Despise their power, and, like a Roman, die." Remains of the castle still stand in Jamaica and many locals believe the ghosts of victims haunt the grounds to this day.[21]

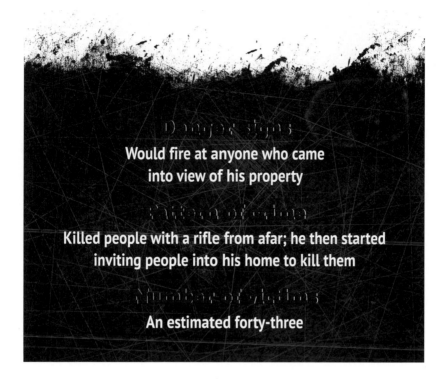

Danger signs
Would fire at anyone who came
into view of his property

Pattern of crime
Killed people with a rifle from afar; he then started
inviting people into his home to kill them

Number of victims
An estimated forty-three

Thug Behram
aka Buhram Jemedar and
the "King of the Thugs"

Born: **1765, date unavailable**
Location: **Central India**
Profession: **Criminal**
Motive: **Gain**
Date of capture: **1840**
Date of death: **1840**

No information is available on Thug Behram's early days, but it is known that as an adult he became a member of the Thuggee cult. This was a group of Hindu and Muslim Indians who worshipped the goddess Kali. Kali is the destructive and creative mother goddess in the Hindu religion. The Thuggee were an organized group of assassins and robbers that spread terror through India as the British presence grew stronger in the country. Members of the cult were called Thugs. (Some say that the English word *thug* comes from Thuggee.) They would often gain the confidence of travelers and then strangle their victims. They believed that during a killing not a single drop of blood should fall on the floor.

Many would kill their victims as Behram did—using the cult's ceremonial cloth called a *rumal*, the Hindi term for handkerchief.

Kali is the Hindu goddess of time, change, creation, preservation, and, most importantly to Thug Behram, power and destruction.

The medallion in the cloth was used to add pressure to the Adam's apple, making it easier to kill. Behram was captured by British authorities. He confessed to his crimes and provided information about the gang. In 1840, at the age of seventy-five, he was hanged. He used his last words to plea for the freedom of his son Ali, who he claimed was never an initiated Thugee.[22,23]

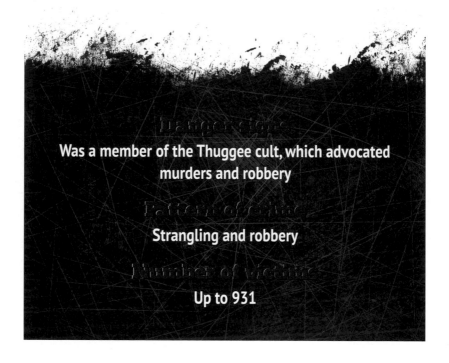

Danger signs

Was a member of the Thuggee cult, which advocated murders and robbery

Pattern of crime

Strangling and robbery

Number of victims

Up to 931

The Harpe Brothers

Born: **1768 (Micajah) and 1770 (Wiley)**

Location: **United States (Tennessee, Kentucky, Illinois, Mississippi)**

Profession: **Criminals**

Motive: **Gain and thrill**

Date of capture: **Big Harpe (August 24, 1799); Little Harpe (January 1804)**

Date of death: **Big Harpe (August 24, 1799); Little Harpe (January 1804)**

In the late 1700s, as the great nation of the United States was being formed, the Harpes were busy killing people. Micajah "Big" Harpe and Wiley "Little" Harpe were the sons of Scottish immigrants in the American colony of North Carolina. They were cousins who grew up together, so they felt like brothers. As boys in 1780, they reportedly decided to fight alongside the British in the Revolutionary War. Micajah was said to be the brawn and Wiley the brains, but both were said to be utterly repugnant. In 1781, after the defeat of the British in Yorktown, the boys left the British army.

By 1781 they had joined with a group of Cherokee Indians and they were raiding villages with them in North Carolina and Tennessee.

For a time, the Harpe brothers lived with Cherokee Indians in the Appalachian Mountains.

They wore buckskins and were rumored to wear scalps as well. Around this time, the brothers decided to get revenge on a Captain James Wood, who had wounded Little Harpe in a previous battle. The brothers kidnapped his daughter, Susan Wood. They also abducted another young woman, Maria Davidson. They forced these women to serve as their wives. When a stranger expressed concern over the welfare of the young women, the Harpes killed him for meddling.

They lived in an Indian village with their abducted wives. Each of their wives had two babies, which the Harpe brothers killed.

They saw children as annoying or inconvenient. In the 1790s, Little Harpe fell in love with a minister's daughter and somehow convinced her to marry him. The Harpes now had three women in their "family." They tried to give up their marauding ways and settle down, building a farm and homestead. However, this was not meant to last. A neighbor, wondering about their three women, got a little too close and the Harpes killed him for his curiosity. By 1798, they were moving around quite a bit and murdering as they went. They enjoyed killing for killing's sake, and anyone who crossed their path became a potential victim. As they moved from Tennessee to Kentucky in the late 1700s, they killed four men. The website Legends of America reports that the brothers seemed more driven by bloodlust than any type of financial gain. After killing their victims, they often disemboweled them, filled their bodies with rocks, and sank them in a river.

When John Langford was found murdered while on a journey from Virginia to Kentucky, the authorities pursued the Harpe brothers. Law enforcement caught the pair and jailed them in Kentucky, but the duo escaped and fled. The public outcry to catch the two grew more than ever, and as the brothers fled their pursuers, dragging their families along, they left a trail of bodies. They killed the young son of a man who had helped police catch them. Then, as they headed north, they killed two more men. When they came upon an encampment along a riverbank, they slayed the three men staying there. A criminal group called the Samuel Mason Gang took them in and they robbed boats moving along the Ohio River. The Harpes would capture travelers, strip them of their clothes, and force them off cliffs. Supposedly, even the ruthless Mason Gang found the Harpe brothers too brutal and asked them to leave.

As they traveled through Tennessee, they killed repeatedly, slashing the throats of men and boys they encountered. They used axes to murder another man and his teenage son. At the home of Moses Stegall, they posed as traveling preachers and were given shelter for the evening. Stegall had a new baby, and when the baby cried in the night, the Harpes slit its throat. They found the baby's mother in the house and killed her as well and then set the house on fire. Stegall joined a posse to track down the ruthless pair. On August 24, 1799, the posse found the pair and asked them to surrender. As the Harpes tried to flee, a posse member shot Big Harpe in the leg and back. Before he died, he confessed to twenty murders. Big Harpe said he and his brother hated humanity and agreed with each other to destroy as many people as they could.

After his confession, Stegall reportedly cut off Big Harpe's head very slowly while he was still alive. His head was hung on a pole in public for years as a warning to other outlaws. Little Harpe rejoined the Mason Gang, but when he heard there was a reward for anyone who brought down the gang leader, he killed Samuel Mason and cut off his head. When he presented the head to authorities, law enforcement recognized Little Harpe and arrested him. He escaped again but was swiftly recaptured. As with Big Harpe, Little Harpe's head was cut off and placed on display along the Natchez Road to serve as warning to any criminals. After their deaths, many families named Harpe or Harper changed their names to erase any association with the cold-blooded killers.[24]

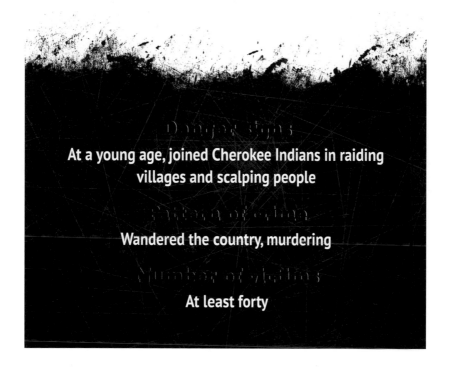

Danger Signs

At a young age, joined Cherokee Indians in raiding villages and scalping people

Pattern of action

Wandered the country, murdering

Number of victims

At least forty

Martha "Patty" Cannon

Born: 1760, date unknown
Location: Sussex County, Delaware
Profession: Slave trader, gang leader
Motive: Gain
Date of capture: 1829
Date of death: May 11, 1829

Martha "Patty" Cannon was born into a life of crime. Her parents were smugglers in Montreal, Canada, and her mother ran a house of prostitution. At age sixteen, Patty married Jesse Cannon, who was a wheelwright. They settled in Delaware and had two children. They were a respectable family. Soon, however, the marriage became strained and Jesse fell ill. After about three years of battling illness, Patty's husband died. Later, she revealed that she had been slowly poisoning him.

With her husband dead, Patty turned to a life of crime. She gathered together a group of criminals and thugs to form a gang of robbers. She was a tough woman whom the thieves respected. Some said that she was strong enough to grab a man by his hair and fling him to the ground and she could take on two men at once in a fight. In time, she opened a tavern with her son-in-law, Joe Johnson, where travelers could stop for a rest and refreshment. If Patty decided a traveler was worth robbing, he would soon be shot or stabbed to death and buried in the yard at the Joe Johnson Tavern.

PATTY CANNON'S HOUSE
AT JOHNSON'S CROSS ROADS WHERE
THE NOTED KIDNAPPING GROUP HAD
HEADQUARTERS AS DESCRIBED IN
GEORGE ALFRED TOWNSEND'S NOVEL
"THE ENTAILED HAT". THE HOUSE
BORDERS ON CAROLINE AND DOR-
CHESTER COUNTIES AND THE STATE
OF DELAWARE.
STATE ROADS COMMISSION

Some locals say that Patty Cannon kidnapped free blacks and sold them into slavery, while others say she kidnapped slaves from one farm and sold them to another.

Patty was always looking to increase her wealth and she saw an opportunity in the slave trade. In 1808, the US Congress banned the importation of slaves. Slavery, however, was still legal in the country and plantation owners wanted them to work their fields. With fewer slaves available because of the ban, the price for slaves rose very high. Many runaway slaves made their way north to the freedom of Delaware. Patty didn't see them as humans, just as valuable property she could capture and sell. She and her thugs began to kidnap black men, women, and children to sell them into slavery. She chained them in hand and leg irons in the attic at Joe Johnson's Tavern and at her home until they could be transported south by covered wagon or sometimes in a large sailing ship called a schooner. If they complained or made noise, they were mercilessly whipped. According to one story, when a five-year-old was having a fit, Patty became enraged and held the child's head over a fire until his face was completely burned.

Even traders seeking to buy slaves were not safe from Patty. According to one story, Patty met a trader she didn't particularly like, who was carrying a lot of cash. She invited him to supper. During the meal she excused herself from the dinner table, snuck back with a gun, and shot the trader dead at the table. She continued her robbing, killing, and slave trading with little trouble from the law. She was arrested for trespassing and assault at one point, but the charges were dropped.

Although people were suspicious of her activities, she lived into her sixties without being discovered. Then, one day a tenant farmer who rented land from Patty was plowing on her property. A small patch of earth gave way under the horse and descended into a hole of loose dirt. When the farmer pulled his horse from the pit, he found a blue chest. Curious, he pried it open and discovered a man's bones inside.

When news of his discovery spread, townspeople were enraged and they thought the rumors of Patty were now confirmed. A mob stormed her house and found a secret room where she had imprisoned freed blacks. Other bodies were found on her property. Now in her sixties, she didn't look like much of a killer, but the evidence proved otherwise. After her arrest, she confessed to killing eleven people and kidnapping slaves. She was officially indicted on four counts of murder for the death of an infant female, a male adult, a male child, and a "Negro" boy. She never went to trial because on May 11, 1829, she was found dead in her cell. It was suspected that she had taken poison. Locals in Delaware spoke of Patty Cannon's ruthless actions for decades and some thought her ghost may still haunt the area. Some parents would warn their children: "Be home before dark or Patty Cannon will get you!"[25,26]

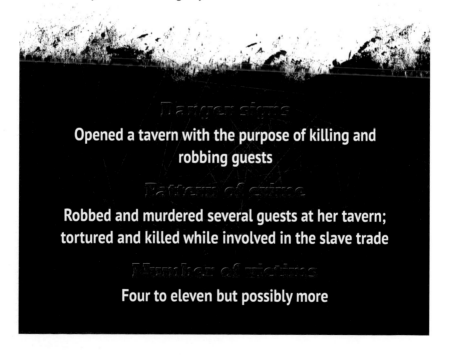

Danger signs

Opened a tavern with the purpose of killing and robbing guests

Pattern of crime

Robbed and murdered several guests at her tavern; tortured and killed while involved in the slave trade

Number of victims

Four to eleven but possibly more

Pierre and Marie Martin

Born: Unknown

Location: Ardèche, France

Profession: Innkeepers

Motive: Gain

Date of capture: November 1, 1831

Date of death: October 2, 1833

L'Auberge Rouge or "The Red Inn" in English is a beautiful country spot located in a remote region of Ardèche, France. It sounds like a peaceful resting place; however, it became the eternal resting place for many who traveled through the region. Originally called *L'Auberge de Peyrebeille,* or the Inn of Peyrebeille, this lodging offered a refuge from the snow and cold that was so common high in the mountains. It is said that Pierre and Marie Martin had trouble making money with their inn, so they decided to kill off guests and take their money and belongings. Apparently, this new approach to innkeeping was quite lucrative and they amassed a fortune of more than half a million dollars.

The husband and wife also enlisted the help of a trusted servant, Jean Rochette (nicknamed *Fetiche* or "Fetish" in English), and Pierre's nephew to carry out the murders. There were claims that they simply knocked their guests over the head, but some say that they gave victims poison as they slept. Rapes and perversions of all kinds

The Inn at Peyrebeille is sometimes called "The Red Inn." It is famous for the crimes committed there between 1807 and 1833.

were said to happen within the cozy confines of the inn. Some claimed that Marie would use bits of the corpses when cooking her patés and stews, which she then fed to new customers. Some reported seeing a hand in a pot, bedsheets and walls stained with blood, and sickening smoke coming from the chimney of The Red Inn. Witnesses assumed this smoke came from the bodies they would burn in their bread oven. Sometimes Marie and Pierre would pretend that they had found a body frozen in the snow.

In October of 1831, a horse dealer went missing. When authorities came to investigate, they found the man dead on the banks of the Allier River with his head smashed in. The horse dealer was last seen at the inn and another man happened to have seen the body being transported via cart from the inn to the river. Pierre, Rochette,

The Martins are rumored to have cut up their victims and fed them to their customers.

the nephew, and Marie were all arrested. Two years later, in June of 1833, the trial of the "four monsters" began. More than a hundred witnesses told stories of disappearances, bodies found, and possible murders. In the end, after seven days of testimony, a judge found all four guilty of just one murder—that of the horse dealer who was found at the river's edge.

The Martins and Rochette were all condemned to death by the guillotine in the courtyard of their inn. On October 2, 1833, a crowd as large as thirty thousand gathered to see the innkeepers have their heads chopped off. The spot is now marked by a stone smeared with a bloody cross. Today, the inn is a tourist attraction from which most return alive.[27]

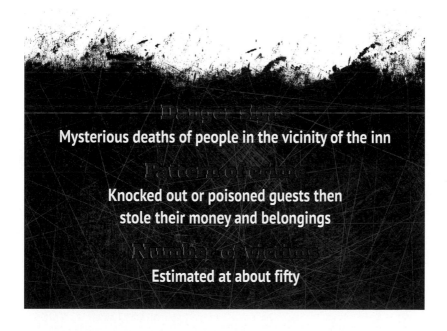

Danger signs

Mysterious deaths of people in the vicinity of the inn

Pattern of crime

Knocked out or poisoned guests then
stole their money and belongings

Number of victims

Estimated at about fifty

Andreas Bichel
aka "The Bavarian Ripper"

Born: 1760, date unknown
Location: Bavaria, Germany
Profession: Fortune-teller, common laborer
Motive: Thrill
Date of capture: May 19, 1808
Date of death: June 9, 1809

In the early 1800s in the Bavarian town of Regendorf, Andreas Bichel was considered an average, unremarkable, but respectable man. Some said he was weak and timid. He was able to work and support his wife, children, and a home. He had a couple of minor crimes on his record—he was once caught stealing vegetables from a neighbor's garden and he also stole some hay from an inn where he worked.

When work with the innkeeper dried up, Bichel thought he'd try his hand at fortune-telling. Taking a magnifying glass and a wooden board, he constructed what he called a magic mirror that could give clients a view into their futures. In 1807, Bichel and his family decided to hire a woman to do some housework. Barbara Reisinger came to interview one day when Bichel's family was out. As they spoke about her housecleaning skills and qualifications, Bichel told Reisinger of his abilities to tell the future. She agreed to try out his magical mirror. Bichel asked Reisinger to sit down facing the "mirror." He told her that the mirror could not show the future if it were touched. To prevent her from touching it, even accidentally, he asked to tie the young woman's hands behind her back. For the mirror to reveal its secrets, she would also have to be blindfolded. Perhaps Reisinger was too trusting, but to all who knew Bichel, he was a harmless man. Obviously, Bichel was now on a different track from the usual. Once the woman was bound and blindfolded, Bichel got a knife and plunged it into her neck. Some claim he severed her spinal cord and stabbed her lungs. He butchered Reisinger while she was still alive. He sliced open her bowels and cracked open her breastbone with a wedge. Once she was dead, he cleaned up and disposed of the body before his family returned home.

When he found that he could get away with such a crime, he tried to repeat it with several other women. Most refused to have their hands tied and left unaware of the danger they had escaped. Then in 1808, a young woman named Catherine Seidel was intrigued by Bichel's magical mirror. He told her to come in her best dress and bring three other dresses, although it's not clear why those other dresses were needed. Seidel suffered the same fate as Reisinger. Bichel disposed of her, and his family remained unaware of his dark side.

Catherine Seidel had a sister, however, who grew concerned when Catherine went missing. She searched for her throughout Regendorf. She happened to go into a tailor's shop and there she found the tailor using fabric that looked just like the material from one of her sister's dresses. The fabric had been sold to the tailor by Andreas Bichel. Catherine's sister told the local police and they immediately went to Bichel. He denied any wrongdoing. He told the authorities that Catherine had met a young man and run off with him.

The police were still suspicious and searched his home. They found some of Catherine's clothing and other women's clothing in his bureau. When a police dog showed interest in Bichel's woodshed, officers entered and uncovered two women's bodies cut in half and a severed head. When the exhumed bodies were laid before him, he confessed all in great detail and with relish. According to ExecutedToday.com, Bichel said he had opened up the women's bodies with a hammer and wedge, breaking through their breast-bones while they were still breathing. What had tipped this mild-mannered man over the edge? He said he was tempted by their fine clothes. On June 9, 1809, Bichel was beheaded.[28,29]

Invited women into his home alone to "see the future"

Tricked women into being alone with him then mutilated their bodies until they died

At least two, possibly up to fifty

William Burke and William Hare

Born: Around 1792

Location: Edinburgh, Scotland

Profession: Laborers, body snatchers

Motive: Gain

Date of capture: November 1, 1828

Date of death: January 28, 1829 (Burke);
1858 (Hare)

Burke and Hare, the two Williams, were friends and hardworking Irishmen laboring in Edinburgh, Scotland. They arrived there from Ireland in about 1827 and moved into the same lodging house, where they became good friends. When an old pensioner died at the lodging house, Burke and Hare decided to take the body to the University of Edinburgh or an anatomy school on Surgeon's Square and sell it. They thought it was only fair because the man had died owing Hare money.

They had heard that medical professors sometimes pay a good price for dead bodies, so they filled the old man's coffin with bark to fool those burying him and took his actual body down to Surgeon's Square. Here they met an assistant to Dr. Robert Knox. Dr. Knox was a skilled surgeon and taught anatomy. He used cadavers to teach students from Edinburgh Medical College about

WILLIAM HARE.
KING'S EVIDENCE

William Hare found that killing people was easier than digging up their bodies.

the body. Burke and Hare received the equivalent of about $1,130 for the cadaver of the old man—a very handsome sum at the time. Dr. Knox was a lecturer who followed the common practice of charging a fee to attend his talks and demonstrations. His lectures drew crowds of medical students and other visitors, sometimes numbering as many as four hundred.

Medical science became a well-established curriculum in the early 1800s. Corpses were essential for training students, but there weren't often enough to meet the demand. Sometimes there were only two or three corpses available a year for a huge group of students. Criminals saw an opportunity to profit from the demand by doctors for bodies. They stole corpses from graves and sold them to colleges (a practice called anatomy murder).

Burke and Hare eagerly sought out their next body. Back at the lodging house, a man named Joseph the Miller was sick. They targeted him as their first murder victim. After sharing some whiskey with him, they suffocated him. Their killing technique of suffocating and compressing the person's chest became known as "burking."

William Burke wanted to provide Dr. Knox with more cadavers.

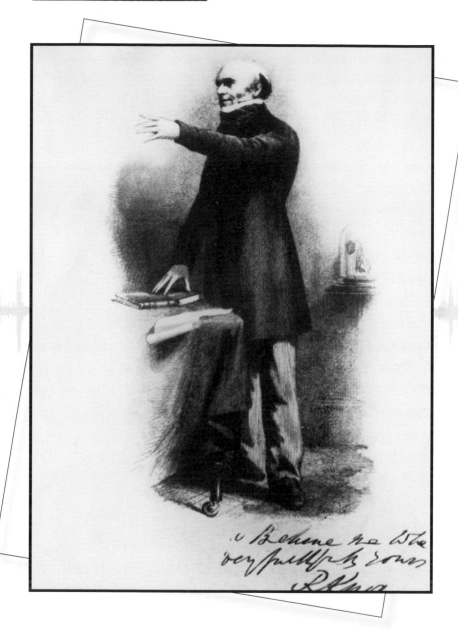

Dr. Knox (1791–1862, shown here ca. 1840) was the head of the Barclay's anatomy school in Edinburgh, Scotland. His reputation was damaged greatly by his involvement with the Williams.

In February of 1828, they invited elderly Abigail Simpson to enjoy some drinks before she had to return to her hometown. When she was intoxicated, they "burked" her, put her in a tea chest, delivered her to Dr. Knox's office, and collected their money.

Hare's wife, Margaret, got in on the action as well. She invited a woman over for drinks and when she was tipsy she told her to visit her husband who dispatched of her. Burke invited two prostitutes—Mary Patterson and Janet Brown—to breakfast. Brown left, however, when an argument upset her. When she later sought out her friend Mary, she couldn't find her. Patterson wound up on the dissecting table, and it is said that some of the students recognized her.

Burke and Hare killed beggars, old women, and even a young blind boy. A woman who hit hard times asked to sleep in a stable run by Hare; she was murdered in the name of science. Later, they murdered that woman's daughter. Many in Edinburgh were familiar with James Wilson, a mentally disabled boy with a limp. He had the nickname Daft Jamie. Burke and Hare targeted Jamie, who was eighteen and rather strong. It took the two of them to subdue and kill the young man. When his body showed up in anatomy class, many students recognized him, but Dr. Knox denied it was Daft Jamie.

A couple of lodgers, James and Ann Gray, found the body of Marjory Campbell Docherty under a bed in the lodging house. They ran to notify the police. By the time the police arrived, Burke and Hare had already removed the corpse and brought it to Dr. Knox. When the police received conflicting stories about the missing woman, they arrested Burke and Hare. The police received a tip that they should visit Dr. Knox and there they found poor Marjory.

Burke and Hare's murder spree lasted one year and left seventeen people dead. Although it seemed clear that Burke and Hare were

Burke and Hare spent a year killing people in order to have bodies to sell to Dr. Knox.

the murderers, the prosecution wasn't sure that the evidence was conclusive. The prosecution decided to offer Hare immunity if he would testify against Burke. Hare's words against his old friend got Burke the death sentence in December of 1828. Burke was hanged on January 28, 1829. Burke swore that Dr. Knox knew nothing of the origin of the cadavers, so Dr. Knox was never prosecuted for any crimes. Reportedly, Dr. Knox continued to use body snatchers.

Burke and Hare figure in many pieces of popular culture. They are the focus of a popular nineteenth-century jump-rope rhyme:

Up the close and down the stair,
But and ben with Burke and Hare.
Burke's the butcher, Hare's the thief,
Knox, the boy who buys the beef. [30,31]

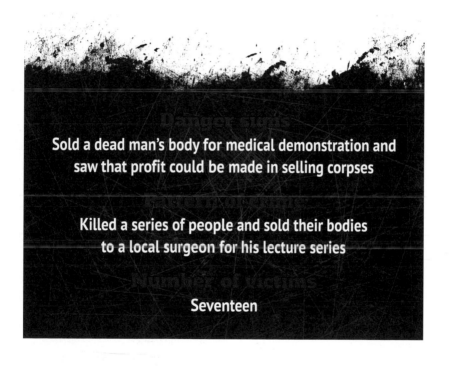

Danger signs

Sold a dead man's body for medical demonstration and saw that profit could be made in selling corpses

Typical victims

Killed a series of people and sold their bodies to a local surgeon for his lecture series

Number of victims

Seventeen

Helene Jegado

Born: 1803, date unknown

Location: Brittany, France

Profession: Domestic servant

Motive: Thrill

Date of capture: July 1, 1851

Date of death: February 26, 1852

Born on a small farm in the province of Brittany in France in the middle of the French Revolution, Helene Jegado lost her mother at age seven and went to live with her aunts. Her aunts worked as servants and at age twenty-three, Jegado began to work in that profession as well. By most accounts, she was a hard worker and there were no signs that she had a killer hidden inside of her. She was accused of stealing a few minor items while employed, but she committed no major crimes.

At age twenty-eight, she shifted paths and joined a convent. Some accounts say that nuns started to get sick after her arrival and a few may have died under suspicious circumstances. Some claim that she started seasoning the nuns' food with arsenic. She volunteered to take care of people; she also enjoyed watching them struggle to stay alive. No deaths of nuns were officially attributed to Jegado.

In 1833, having renounced her habit she went to work for a priest. Father François Le Drogo lived in the village of Guern.

Less than three months after Jegado was hired, the priest, his elderly parents, and three others in the household all died. Jegado's sister, who was visiting her at the time, also died. Jegado's tears flowed and she showed such sorrow at the loss that she was not considered a suspect. There had been a cholera epidemic at this time, so most people thought the deaths were due to a disease of some sort.

Jegado's sister had been working as a servant and Jegado offered to take her place after her death. Woe came to the family that hired her. Three people died while she was employed there, including her aunt. She tended to each by their bedside and was grief-stricken each time one died. Although death appeared to follow her, she always found work. In her next job, doing needlework for a family, a mother and daughter took ill and passed away. The son got sick but refused Jegado's care and managed to live. Jegado took a room with an old widow and offered to cook her soup. The broth led to the widow's untimely demise. In 1835, a Madame Toussaint hired the seemingly pious Jegado. Jegado was overcome with sorrow when four in that household were buried. She went from household to household, town to town, leaving a trail of bodies along the way. In May 1841, a child who was in her care died, but again she was not accused.

Then, for a stretch of about ten years, Jegado aparently did not poison anyone. Perhaps she was happy with her new employers or needed a break. But by 1850, Jegado was back to her old ways. Soon after a professor of law at the University of Rennes hired her, a maid in the household fell ill. Jegado tended to her until she died. Another maid became ill with the same symptoms. As with the first, doctors were called in to try to save her but to no avail. After this second maid died, the doctors recommended that an autopsy be performed.

Before anyone even considered Jegado a suspect, she told the family she was innocent of any wrongdoing. This aroused suspicion and she was arrested July 1, 1851. Upon examination of her most recent victims, the doctors found arsenic in their systems. French law had a statute of limitations on crimes, so Jegado was tried for just three murders and three attempted murders. She was executed by guillotine before a large crowd on February 26, 1852.[32,33]

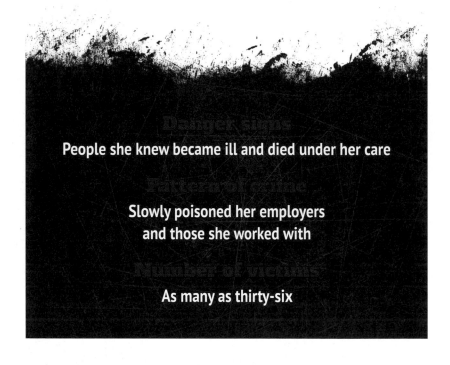

Danger signs

People she knew became ill and died under her care

Pattern of crime

Slowly poisoned her employers
and those she worked with

Number of victims

As many as thirty-six

Manuel Blanco Romasanta

aka "The Werewolf of Allariz" or "The Tallow Man"

Born: **November 18, 1809**

Location: **Galicia, Spain**

Profession: **Tailor**

Motive: **Thrill**

Date of capture: **September 1852**

Date of death: **December 14, 1863**

Born on November 18, 1809, Manuel Blanco Romasanta was born in the small village of Regueiro. At birth, Manuel's parents thought he was a girl and named him Manuela. Not until age six did a doctor discover his true sex. According to some reports, he was raised as a female and had a small build. Even as a grown man, he reportedly was just under five feet (1.5 meters) tall. Some believe his family was fairly well off because Romasanta could read and write at a young age.

He settled into a career as a tailor as a young man and married. After his wife died, when he was just twenty-four, he decided to become a traveling salesman. He roamed widely through Galicia (northern Spain), Castile (which stretches from the north through central and southwestern Spain), and Portugal. He also worked as a guide for those journeying through certain mountainous areas of Spain. Romasanta appeared to be living a stable, productive life until 1844.

In that year, a constable named Vicente Fernandez from the northwestern Spanish city of León came to Romasanta to collect a debt of 600 reales (Spanish currency). He owed the money to one of his merchandise suppliers. That officer was soon found dead and evidence pointed to Romasanta. He was asked to appear before a court but did not show up. For failing to appear in court, he was automatically sentenced to ten years in prison.

Now wanted by the law, Romasanta fled to the small village of Rebordechao, just north of the Portuguese border. He assumed the false identity of Antonio Gomez. For a while, it seems that he lived a productive life and was appreciated by the community. He worked making cord and harvesting crops. As described in the book *The Murder Stories* by Kristen Laurence, Romasanta became very friendly with the women of the village. Some thought of him as effeminate because he spent a good deal of time spinning yarn and cooking with the ladies of the area.

Villagers were aware that Romasanta had traveled extensively and worked as a guide. A group of women and children hired him to escort them to distant locations, and somewhere along the way seven women and two children disappeared. To avoid suspicion, Romasanta delivered letters to their families in Rebordechao, which implied their loved ones had arrived safely at their destinations and were settling in. However, when he started selling the clothing of his victims, many suspected that he had killed the travelers.

Some claimed that Romasanta also sold candles made of human fat, which earned him the nickname of "The Tallow Man."

A formal complaint was filed against him in Escalona accusing him of murder and pursuing his grotesque craft of making candles from human bodies.

In September 1852, Romasanta was arrested in Toledo and brought to trial in the town of Allariz. He confessed to killing thirteen people, but he had an unusual defense. He said he could not help himself because he was afflicted with lycanthropy (the supernatural transformation of a human into animal). The trial lasted seven months. He testified to the court:

> *The first time I transformed, was in the mountains of Couso. I came across two ferocious-looking wolves. I suddenly fell to the floor, and began to feel convulsions, I rolled over three times, and a few seconds later I myself was a wolf. I was out marauding with the other two for five days, until I returned to my own body, the one you see before you today, Your Honour. The other two wolves came with me, who I thought were also wolves, changed into human form. They were from Valencia. One was called Antonio and the other Don Genaro. They too were cursed ... We attacked and ate a number of people because we were hungry.*

He was asked to transform to prove before the court that he was indeed a werewolf, but he explained that the curse on him had only lasted thirteen years and it had just ended.

Romasanta was found guilty of nine of the murders; the court determined that the other four were actually the work of wolves. He was sentenced on August 6, 1853, to be executed by garrote (a wire with a handle on each end, used to strangle a person). A French hypnotist was convinced that Romasanta was not guilty because he was suffering from a mental condition that made him believe he was a werewolf. At the time, that area of Spain was going through a horrible famine that was said to drive some people mad and possibly drive some to drastic measures. He thought he could cure Romasanta and asked the Minister of Justice for time to study him. The Minister of Justice told Queen Isabella II of the request, and she changed Romasanta's punishment from death to life imprisonment. Still, Romasanta died in prison just a few months later.[34,35]

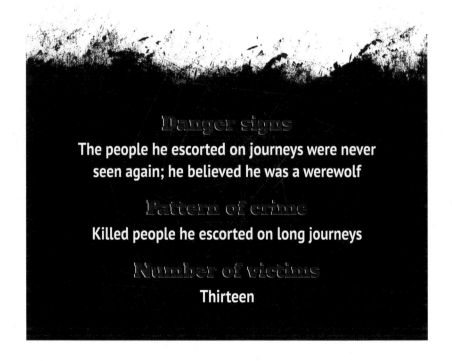

Danger signs
The people he escorted on journeys were never seen again; he believed he was a werewolf

Pattern of crime
Killed people he escorted on long journeys

Number of victims
Thirteen

John Johnston

aka "Liver-Eating Johnson" or "Crow Killer"

Born: **1824**

Location: **Northern Rockies and the plains of Wyoming and Montana**

Profession: **Fur trapper and hunter**

Motive: **Power and revenge**

Date of capture: **Never arrested**

Date of death: **January 21, 1900**

Born in New Jersey, John Garrison grew up to be a six-foot (1.8-m) tall, 260-pound (118-kilogram) strapping, muscular young man that wouldn't be messed with. He enlisted in the US Navy to fight in the Mexican-American War but deserted after striking a superior officer. To avoid being brought up on charges, Garrison changed his name to John Johnston (sometimes Johnson) and rode the rails west. He eventually met up with a man called Old John Hatcher. In northern Colorado on the Little Snake River, Old John taught Johnston how to trap, hunt, and survive in the wild.

Growing a full red beard and wearing buckskin, Johnston became an authentic mountain man, expert with both the rifle and the Bowie knife. Johnston did business with local Indians, and in one of these trades he was offered the daughter of a Flathead Indian chief. He took

A bronze statue was erected over Liver-Eating Johnston's grave at Old Trail Town in Cody, Wyoming.

the woman as his wife and by all accounts he fell in love. He asked his wife to teach him her tribe's native language so that he could show his respect for her. Before going on a winter hunting expedition one year, he taught his wife how to handle a rifle. He headed off for months and looked forward to the spring, when he would see his wife again.

When Johnston returned to his cabin after the winter of 1847, he found a gruesome scene. His wife had been brutally slaughtered and her remains lay in the doorway to their home. Then he saw something more horrific: ripped from her gut was the skin and bones of a small infant. It was Johnston's child. From the traces left behind, he realized that the killing was the coldhearted work of the Crow Indians. Johnston was blind with rage and swore vengeance against all Crow Indians.

Soon after, the Rocky Mountains and the plains of Montana and Wyoming were littered with the bodies of Crow—scalped and with livers removed. Some claim that Johnston had eaten the livers of the Indian warriors. This act was significant because the Crow believed that the liver was necessary for one to go on in the afterlife.

One remarkable story in J. P. Walker's book *The Legendary Mountain Men of North America* tells how Blackfoot Indians captured Johnston. They planned to sell him to the Crow. They stripped him to the waist and tied him up inside a teepee with an inexperienced guard standing watch outside. Johnston was able to wriggle free. He killed and scalped the guard. He also cut off the guard's leg so he would have something to eat as he fled into the woods. In one account, the Crow tribe sent twenty of its best warriors to track and kill Johnston. Not one returned alive. It is said that he killed, scalped, and ate the livers of up to three hundred Crow warriors.

Crow warriors were known for being particularly brutal. John "Liver-Eating" Johnston murdered many Crows in retribution for the deaths of his wife and child.

After twenty years, Johnston made peace with the Crow and he even called them his brothers. In his forties, he joined the Union army and fought in the Civil War as a sharpshooter. Later in his life, he shed his mountain man ways. He became a respected deputy sheriff in the town of Leadville, Colorado, and eventually a marshal in Red Lodge, Montana. In December 1899 at the age of seventy-six, he was admitted to the hospital. A month later, at the turn of the century, Johnston died.[36,37]

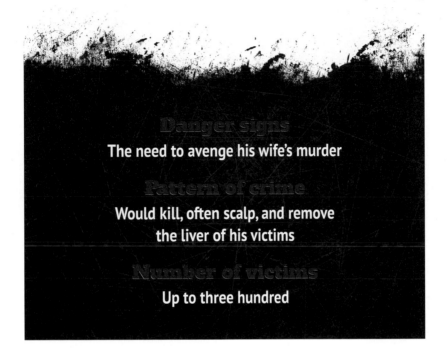

Danger signs

The need to avenge his wife's murder

Pattern of crime

Would kill, often scalp, and remove
the liver of his victims

Number of victims

Up to three hundred

Born: **May 16, 1861**

Location: **Chicago, Illinois**

Profession: **Pharmacy owner and hotel owner**

Motives: **Gain and thrill**

Date of capture: **November 17, 1894**

Date of death: **May 7, 1896**

Herman Webster Mudgett was born in Gilmanton, New Hampshire, into a wealthy family. Stories of his youth give us some insight into his lurid future. According to one account, Mudgett was bullied as a young boy. One day, fellow students took him to a doctor's office. They forced him to touch a skeleton to creep him out. Instead, he found the human remains fascinating. He told family that he was interested in medicine and he practiced crude surgery on animals. Some believe that he was responsible for the death of a friend when he was only a child. His behavior and inclinations seemed to foreshadow the large-scale and ghastly crimes to come.

Yet, on the surface, Mudgett pursued a respectable life course. He married Clara Lovering in 1878 and they had a son. In 1882, he entered medical school at the University of Michigan. Here, his taste for crime and the macabre became apparent. He discovered the

H. H. Holmes is considered America's first serial killer.

identities of the corpses in his labs and then took out life insurance policies in their names. He figured out a way to disfigure the bodies, claim they had died in accidents, and collect on the policies as the next of kin.

After he graduated from medical school, he moved to Chicago and created the false identity of Dr. Henry Howard Holmes. Perhaps he made the alias so he could marry another woman without divorcing his first wife. In 1887, after abandoning his first family, he married Myrta Belknap and they had a daughter. He later also married Georgiana Yoke in Denver, Colorado, without ever divorcing his first two wives. In Chicago, he found work in a pharmacy. The owners respected him for his hard work, and he eventually bought the pharmacy.

When the opportunity arose to buy a lot across the street, he jumped at it. Here, Holmes built the World's Fair Hotel, a place where people could stay during the World's Columbian Exposition, also known as the Chicago World's Fair of 1893. The Exposition opened on May 1 and for the next six months, more than twenty-six million visitors would come for the food, entertainment, and the presentation of the latest technological gadgets. Holmes thought he'd make money from hotel guests, but his plans for his building were more insidious. He called his structure the "Castle." The three-story hotel was built as an elaborate maze that only Holmes understood. He hired a series of different workmen and carpenters so no one saw a full picture of what he was building.

The first floor had normal shops and Holmes resided on the top floor, but the middle floor featured rooms that were windowless, soundproof, and locked only from the outside. Many walls in the hotel rooms were equipped with gas jets, which Holmes would later use to asphyxiate his victims. With the press of a button, Holmes could kill people while he sat comfortably in his office. Rooms were built with secret trapdoors and chutes. This was so bodies could be easily dropped into the basement, where he would burn them or dispose of them in acid or dissect them and prepare them for sale to medical schools. There were also inexplicable doorways opening to brick walls and hallways leading to nowhere. Later, his hotel would be nicknamed the Murder Castle and reveal how clever and monstrous he truly was.

601–603 W. 63rd Street in Chicago took up an entire city block and would come to be called the "Murder Castle."

By all accounts, Holmes was an adept swindler. He was clever with his speech, confident, seemingly business savvy, and successful at wooing women. When the young, attractive, and married Julia Connor came to work for him as a bookkeeper, Holmes seduced her. Julia's husband left her and their daughter, Pearl, when he found out about the affair. Julia and Pearl moved in with Holmes, and soon Julia became pregnant. Holmes took out life insurance policies on both Julia and Pearl, and a short time thereafter both were found dead under mysterious circumstances.

At his hotel, he would kill for pleasure and sometimes for gain. He had implements of torture, including a torture rack that he used to force people to sign over their wealth and property. He forced women to write to their relatives explaining that they'd gone away so their disappearance would not raise suspicion. Some victims may have been burned alive in rooms. In the book *Serial Killing for Profit: Multiple Murder for Money*, author Dirk Gibson recounts how Holmes left one woman sealed in a soundproof chamber where she cried and screamed for days until she died of starvation.

No one is sure of the total number of people who were killed in the Murder Castle, but it could have been in the hundreds. Holmes, who was in constant trouble with creditors, fled Chicago after the Exhibition ended, killing others along the way. While at the hotel, he had formed a bond with a Benjamin Pietzel, who helped him with many of his horrific plans. Holmes treated Pietzel like his puppet. He called him his tool and his creature. After abandoning the hotel, Holmes convinced Pietzel to take out a life insurance policy on himself. He told Pietzel they would fake his death and split the payout. Instead of faking his death, however, Holmes simply killed him and collected on the policy. Pietzel's wife knew about her husband's plan to fake his death. Holmes met with her and convinced her that he was still alive and would return soon. Holmes also persuaded Pietzel's wife that he should keep three of their five children safe with him until Pietzel returned. Once Holmes had these children, he decided to kill them as well. He buried two of the children in a basement of the home he rented and stuffed the third child's body in a chimney. On November 17, 1894, Holmes was finally arrested. On May 7, 1896, Holmes was executed by hanging at Moyamensing Prison in Philadelphia.[38,39,40]

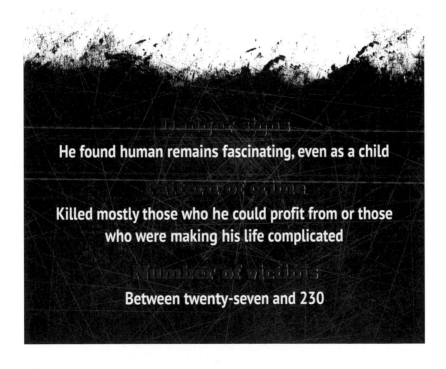

He found human remains fascinating, even as a child

Killed mostly those who he could profit from or those who were making his life complicated

Between twenty-seven and 230

Jack the Ripper

Born: Nineteenth century
Location: London, England
Profession: Unknown
Motive: Unknown
Date of capture: Never captured
Date of death: Unknown

From August 7 until September 10, 1888, a mysterious villain prowled the streets of London after dark, killing five prostitutes in the gritty, crime-filled White Chapel neighborhood. The murders were notable for their brutality. All the victims had been strangled, throats cut, and then bodies mutilated. Police discovered that most were disemboweled and sometimes organs were missing. His nickname came from this killing method and from letters written to the police by someone who claimed to be the murderer. The letters were sent to Scotland Yard, taunting the authorities about their inability to catch him and boasting of his repulsive crimes, as well as those to come.

His first victim, Mary Ann "Polly" Nichols, was found with an eight-inch (20-centimeter) cut along the throat as well as violent lacerations to the abdomen. A witness spotted the second prostitute victim with a man who was described only as a "shabby gentile."

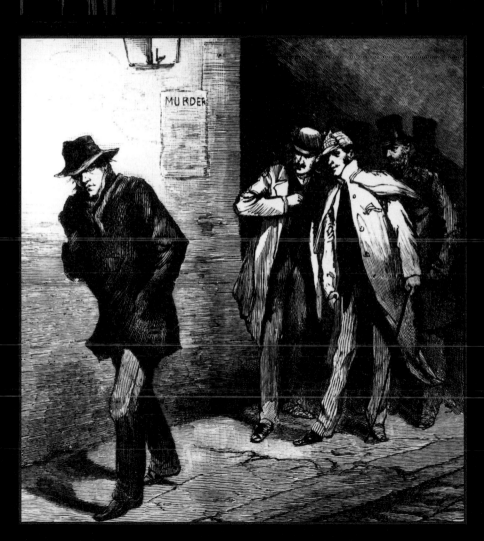

Jack the Ripper had all of London on high alert, especially the police.

That woman, Annie Chapman, ended up in back of an apartment building, strangled, her throat cut, and disemboweled with her intestines placed on her shoulder. Another target was cut open from rectum to sternum. On September 30, 1888, he killed two women in one night.

The final prostitute was the most brutally mutilated. Mary Jane Kelly, a pretty twenty-five-year-old, had her face cut so extensively it was almost gone. She was stabbed in the neck with a knife that cut to the vertebrae. Her breasts and organs were carved out and placed in a pile by the body. Part of her heart was removed. Slices of flesh were placed on her nightstand.

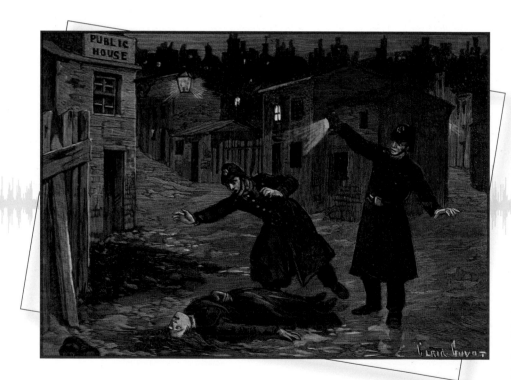

The murder of Mary Jane Kelly was particularly vicious.

Although the Ripper was never caught, several men were suspected. One was a deranged Polish barber named Aaron Kosminski. In the 1880s, he was in his early twenties and working in the East End as a hairdresser. Local police said he had a great hatred of women and homicidal tendencies, which led to his commitment in a lunatic asylum. Other suspects included a petty thief, a surgeon who worked as a hairdresser in London and later poisoned two of his wives, and a doctor who was found dead in the Thames River about three months after the final killing.[41]

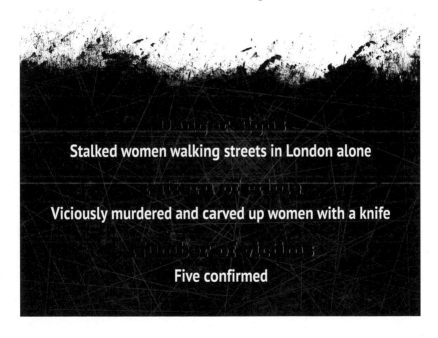

Stalked women walking streets in London alone

Viciously murdered and carved up women with a knife

Five confirmed

The Bender Family
aka *"The Blood Benders"*

Born: The nineteenth century, ranging in age from twenty-two to sixty

Location: Labette County, Kansas

Profession: General store owners and innkeepers

Diagnosis: Gain and possibly thrill

Date of capture: Never captured

Date of death: Unknown

"Going on a bender" is an expression that means to go overboard drinking alcohol. In southeast Kansas, however, it has a more sinister meaning because of the evildoings of the Bender family, who once lived in this area. Most tales of serial killing involve a solitary person, but for the Benders, murder was a family affair. In 1872, John Bender Sr. was about sixty, Ma Bender was forty-two, their son John was twenty-five, and their daughter Kate was twenty-two. After the Civil War ended in 1865, land out West was opened to homesteaders. Those who wanted to move westward and get property for free could do so, if they agreed to settle there. The Benders moved to Labette County, Kansas, and built a combination home/grocery store/inn.

Their little house on the prairie turned out to be a little house of horrors. Ma and Pa Bender had emigrated to the United States from

Germany and they maintained such strong accents that people had trouble understanding the couple. John Jr. was considered dim-witted. Kate, however, was a bit of a star. The young beauty performed in nearby towns as a spiritualist. She said she could contact the dead and even heal the sick. Men especially liked the performances by the attractive Kate. Some would even purposely stay at the Benders' inn to see her. Unfortunately, some of those men were never seen again.

If an inn visitor appeared to have money, the family might invite him to dinner, or they might treat him to a spiritual session. The place of honor at the table was a chair that positioned the guest with his back against a canvas wall. Kate would distract the guest and then at just the right moment, Pa or John Jr. would whack the customer on the head with a sledgehammer or cut his throat. Their victim would be stripped of valuables and then his body thrown

The beautiful Kate Bender would lure guests to her family home, where her father or brother would kill them for their valuables. Their home was the site of many brutal deaths.

down a trapdoor and into an earthen cellar. They would later bury the body farther away from the inn.

Over the course of a year, so many people went missing from the area that many began to avoid that part of Kansas. In the spring of 1873, a Dr. William York came to stay at the inn and possibly visit with the lovely Kate. Dr. York wound up in the cellar like so many others. A short while later, his brother Colonel York came in search of William. The Benders said they hadn't seen him at all. Colonel York believed them and took a room for the night. While sitting in a room before bed, Colonel York noticed something glittering on the floor under some furniture. He discovered that it was a locket and chain belonging to his brother. York decided to slip out and contact the authorities. As he quietly left, he saw a light in a nearby orchard. He snuck over to investigate and he saw old Pa Bender burying something wrapped in canvas. York swore that it had to be a body. York hightailed it to town to get a group of law officers to come and investigate the scene.

When they returned, all the Benders were gone. York and the others scoured the grounds and found eleven graves—one held William York. When they examined the inn, they saw the setup with the canvas and trapdoor and found dried blood on the floor and in the earthen cellar. After hearing stories from a few who had escaped the inn, the authorities pieced together how the men had been killed. The State of Kansas offered a $2,000 reward to anyone who could apprehend the murderous clan, but the Bender family was never seen again.[42,43]

Danger Signs

Disappearing inn guests

Pattern of action

Hit unsuspecting guests with sledgehammer;
dispose of bodies through a trapdoor

Number of victims

At least eleven

Earle Leonard Nelson
aka "The Gorilla Killer"

Born: May 12, 1897

Location: United States and Canada

Profession: Drifter and petty thief

Motive: Lust

Date of capture: June 10, 1927

Date of death: January 13, 1928

When Earle Leonard Nelson was just a young boy, both his parents died of venereal disease and he went to live with his aunt. His aunt was a religious zealot, and Nelson would develop his own odd obsession with religion. After a streetcar hit him while he was riding his bicycle at age ten, he developed physical and mental problems. At fourteen, he was admitted to a mental hospital after trying to rape a neighbor's daughter. He enlisted in the US Navy, but he spent his days lying on his cot and ranting about "The Great Beast of Revelations." The military committed him to a mental institution once again. Eventually, he was discharged and set free.

When he was just twenty-two, he met a woman twice his age and married her. It is said that his sexual perversion and extreme jealousy drove her to a nervous breakdown. In February 1926, something seemed to snap within Nelson and his behavior became more violent.

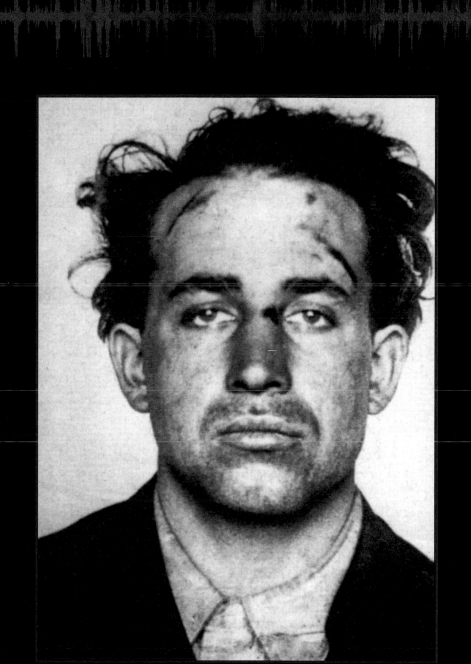

For sixteen months, Nelson traveled around the United States and eventually into Canada, murdering women, most of them widows or unmarried landladies. The women accepted him into their homes because he was mild-mannered, had a gentle smile, and carried a Bible with him everywhere. He typically raped and then strangled each of his victims.

Because he kept moving, Nelson eluded police. He murdered women up and down the West Coast, in Iowa, Missouri, New York, Michigan, and Illinois. Police pieced together a description of a man with large hands, protruding lips, and a small forehead. His physical features, combined with the animal force of his attacks, earned him the nickname "the Gorilla Killer."

In June 1927, Nelson made his way to Winnipeg, Canada, where he strangled a fourteen-year-old girl and then bludgeoned a house-wife and stuffed her body under a bed. He stole some of her clothing and sold it to a used-clothing store. With some cash in hand, he went to the barber. The barber noticed blood in his hair, and he thought he recognized Nelson from a Wanted poster. The barber called the police, and Nelson was picked up shortly thereafter.

For his murders in Canada, Nelson was put on trial on November 1, 1927. He was hanged on January 13, 1928.[44]

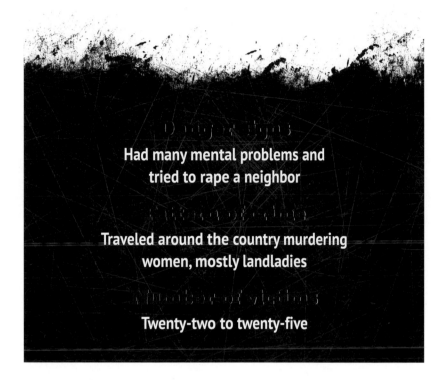

Had many mental problems and
tried to rape a neighbor

Traveled around the country murdering
women, mostly landladies

Twenty-two to twenty-five

Albert Fish
aka "The Gray Man," "The Werewolf of Wysteria," or "The Brooklyn Vampire"

Born: May 19, 1870
Location: United States
Profession: House painter, handyman
Motive: Thrill and sadomasochism
Date of capture: December 13, 1934
Date of death: January 16, 1936

From an early age, Albert Fish had a strange attraction to pain. After his father died when he was five years old, his mother put him in an orphanage. The workers there would occasionally beat him, which he found pleasurable. At age twelve, he would go to public baths to watch other boys undress. At twenty, Fish moved to New York City from Washington, DC, and became a male prostitute. In 1898, at age twenty-eight, he seemed to pull his life together to some degree. He met a woman, got married, and had six children. He worked mostly as a handyman and painter to support the family.

In January 1917, when Fish was forty-seven, his wife left him for another man. That's when his children noticed a change in him. He started to take them to a family cottage in Westchester County, New York. Here, he would scream at the sky that he was

Albert Fish was a particularly troubled individual. Not only did he abuse and eat his victims, but he also regularly molested children and beat himself.

Jesus Christ. He asked the neighbor's children to beat his backside with a paddle studded with nails until he bled. He burned himself with hot irons and pokers and stuck needles into his body. In his search for a new wife, he answered classified ads from women seeking husbands. But his replies were often about his wish to be paddled and not a wish to fall in love. On full moons, he would eat large quantities of raw meat. He read extensively about cannibalism. He went to a few psychiatrists, but they always sent him on his way with an evaluation of being disturbed but sane.

When he was later caught, this assessment was proved dead wrong. He confessed to molesting hundreds and killing several children.

When he was fifty-eight, Fish committed a clever, brutal, and grotesque murder that would eventually bring him to justice. In the May 28, 1928, issue of a New York newspaper, Fish spotted an ad from an eighteen-year-old boy looking for work in the country. Fish thought he might be able to take advantage of this boy so he went to the address provided, in the Manhattan neighborhood of Chelsea. The boy was Edward Budd, and he invited in the aging, gray-haired Albert Fish when he knocked at the door. Fish presented himself to Budd's family as "Frank Howard," a farmer from Long Island. He was introduced to Edward's parents and Edward's younger sister, the ten-year-old Grace. Fish told the family he would hire the boy for fifteen dollars a week, and he would return next week to fetch Edward for the job. The family was elated. In reality, Fish was sizing up Edward to see if he would be a suitable victim. He quickly realized that Edward was too big for him to overpower, but when he met his young sister, Fish saw a potential new victim.

About a week later, he arrived at lunchtime with strawberries and cheese. He charmed the family with his good manners. He held Grace on his lap. She kissed him and he decided he wanted to eat her. He told the family that he would take Edward with him to the farm that night but first he had to attend a special children's birthday party in uptown Manhattan that afternoon—a party that he thought young Grace would enjoy. He suggested that Grace come with him as a treat. He'd bring her back later that day and then Edward and he would depart for his farm. Grace's parents thought that was awfully kind of him and let her go with Albert.

Albert Fish was caught because he boasted about his crime to his victim's parents.

Police officers found the remains of several children buried on Fish's property.

Albert's real plan was terribly sinister. He took the child with him to his cabin in Westchester. He carried along a package containing a meat cleaver, a butcher knife, and a saw. He almost left the package behind on the train, but the young, trusting Grace thoughtfully reminded him to take it. They went to his cottage where he told Grace to play in the yard. Fish went into the house and got completely naked. When he called the young girl in he killed her, chopped her up, and proceeded to eat her over the course of nine days.

When the girl did not return as promised, the parents were devastated. Police conducted an extensive manhunt for the elderly gentleman who had kidnapped her but did not get any leads. It was six years before the police found their man. The break came when Fish sent the Budd family a letter describing in revolting detail what he had done to young Grace. The stationary gave a small clue to who wrote the letter and eventually led to Albert Fish. Fish gave all the details of this crime and others. Police found Grace's remains at the cottage. On January 16, 1936, the sixty-six-year-old Albert Fish was put to death in the electric chair—one of the oldest men to ever be executed by electrocution.[45]

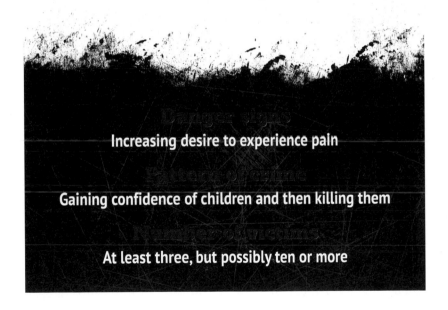

Danger signs

Increasing desire to experience pain

Pattern of crime

Gaining confidence of children and then killing them

Number of victims

At least three, but possibly ten or more

CONCLUSION

Looking back hundreds of years, we see that there have always been people interested in killing others for some sort of perverse thrill and without empathy toward the victim. Luckily, serial killers make up a very small percentage of the entire population of the world, but their stories fascinate us because it can be difficult to understand how anyone who is human can commit such horrific acts.

Throughout history we get some indication of how people become serial killers. Elizabeth Báthory, or "The Blood Countess," had an aunt who showed her the pleasures of inflicting pain on others. With Albert Fish, we see how losing his father and going to an orphanage may have fostered his tastes for perversion. Earle Leonard Nelson, "The Gorilla Killer," had a head injury as a child that may have triggered his murderous ways. Perhaps it damaged the orbital cortex, which is believed to be a common factor among killers.

Serial killing appears to be as old as mankind itself and understanding the behaviors, motivations, and triggers for these horrendous acts may help prevent history from repeating itself.

Psychopathy Quiz

Are You a Psychopath?

This quiz is designed to help give you some insight into people with psychopathic tendencies. While the quiz is not meant to diagnose psychopathy, it may also give you an idea about whether or not *you* have such tendencies.

Read each of the following statements and answer each honestly. Give yourself two points if the statement definitely describes you, one point if it somewhat describes you, and zero points if it doesn't describe you at all. Tally up the points to see where *you* sit on the psychopathy scale!

1. I'd rather be spontaneous than make plans.
2. I wouldn't have a problem cheating on a boyfriend or girlfriend if I knew I could get away with it.
3. I don't mind ditching plans to hang out with my friends if something better comes along—like a chance to go out with that hot new guy or girl.
4. Seeing animals injured or in pain doesn't bother me.
5. I love excitement and danger.
6. I think it's OK to manipulate others so that I can get ahead.
7. I'm a smooth talker: I can always get people to do what I want them to do.
8. I'm great at making quick decisions.
9. I don't get it when movies or TV shows make people cry.

10. Most people just bring problems upon themselves, so why should I help them?

11. I'm rarely to blame when things go wrong—it's others who are incompetent, not me.

12. I have more talent in the tip of my little finger than most people will ever have.

13. I am able to make other people believe my lies.

14. I don't feel guilty when I make people feel bad.

15. I often borrow things and then lose or forget to return them.

16. I skip school or work more than most people I know.

17. I tend to blurt out exactly what's on my mind.

18. I often get into trouble because I lie a lot.

19. I skip school and/or often don't get my assignments done on time.

20. I think that crying is a sign of weakness.

If you scored 30–40 points, you have many psychopath tendencies.

If you scored 20–39 points, you have some psychopathic tendencies.

If you scored 0–19 points, you have no psychopathic tendencies.

Chapter Notes

Introduction

1. Scott Bonn, *Why We Love Serial Killers: The Curious Appeal of the World's Most Savage Murderers* (New York: Skyhorse Publishing, 2014).
2. Joanne Ostrow, "Dexter, Hannibal, Bates Motel: Why Do We Love TV Serial Killers?" *The Denver Post*, February, 9, 2014, http://www.denverpost.com/television/ci_25079885/dexter-hannibal-bates-motel-why-do-we-love.
3. Scott Bonn, "5 Myths about Serial Killers and Why They Persist [Excerpt]," *Scientific American*, October 24, 2014, http://www.scientificamerican.com/article/5-myths-about-serial-killers-and-why-they-persist-excerpt/.
4. "Some 437,000 People Murdered Worldwide in 2012, According to New UNODC Study," The United Nations Office of Drugs and Crime, April 2014, https://www.unodc.org/unodc/en/press/releases/2014/April/some-437000-people-murdered-worldwide-in-2012-according-to-new-unodc-study.html.
5. Scott Bonn, "5 Myths about Serial Killers and Why They Persist [Excerpt]."
6. Christopher Beam, "Blood Loss: The Decline of the Serial Killer," *Slate*, January 5, 2011, http://www.slate.com/articles/news_and_politics/crime/2011/01/blood_loss.html.
7. "Serial Murder: Multi-Disciplinary Perspectives for Investigators," The Federal Bureau of Investigation, https://www.fbi.gov/stats-services/publications/serial-murder.
8. Katherine Ramsland, "Who Coined 'Serial Killer'?" *Psychology Today*, October 11, 2014, https://www.psychologytoday.com/blog/shadow-boxing/201410/who-coined-serial-killer.

Chapter 1: Types of Serial Killers

1. Meredith Galante, "There Are Two Types of Serial Killers and It's Easy to Tell Them Apart," *Business Insider*, April 12, 2012, http://www.businessinsider.com/types-of-serial-killers-2012-4.
2. "Types of Serial Killers," The Crime Museum, http://www.crimemuseum.org/crime-library/types-of-serial-killers.
3. "Holmes Typology," Serial Killers Defined, http://twistedminds.creativescapism.com/serial-killers-introduction/holmes-typology/.

4. Deborah Schurman-Kauflin, "Why Cannibals Love Eating People," *Psychology Today*, August 30, 2011, https://www.psychologytoday.com/blog/disturbed/201108/why-cannibals-love-eating-people.

Chapter 2: Causes and Characteristics of Serial Killers

1. Julia Layton, "How Did Forensics Experts Create a Modern Profile of Jack the Ripper?" HowStuffWorks.com, http://history.howstuffworks.com/history-vs-myth/ripper-profile.htm.
2. Kira Dawn Wissman, "Nature Vs. Nurture: Serial Killers and Social Psychology," *Applied Social Psychology*, October 20, 2013, http://www.personal.psu.edu/bfr3/blogs/asp/2013/10/nature-vs-nurture-serial-killers-and-social-psychology.html.
3. Jim Fallon, "Exploring the Mind of a Killer," *TED Talk*, July 2009.
4. "Analysis of Nature Vs. Nurture," *Nature Vs. Nurture*, October 22, 2009, http://scienceiscool25.blogspot.com/2009/10/analysis-of-nature-vs-nurture-updated.html.
5. "The Psychology of a Serial Killer," Le Moyne College, http://web.lemoyne.edu/~Freemams/index_files/psych_serial.htm.
6. Katherine Ramsland, "Triad of Evil," *Psychology Today*, March 16, 2012, https://www.psychologytoday.com/blog/shadow-boxing/201203/triad-evil.

Chapter 3: Profiles of Serial Killers Throughout History

1. Ann Wamack, "Locusta of Gaul, Roman 'Herbalist' and Professional Poisoner," Historyswomen.com, http://www.historyswomen.com/moregreatwomen/Locusta.html.
2. "Joan of Arc," Bio, http://www.biography.com/people/joan-of-arc-9354756.
3. "Gilles de Rais," *Encyclopaedia Brittannica*, Updated September 9, 2013, http://www.britannica.com/biography/Gilles-de-Rais.
4. "Gilles de Rais—Famous Serial Killer," HellHorror.com, http://hellhorror.com/serial-killer-55/Gilles-de-Rais.html.

5. Alex Anderson, "Liu Pengli: The First Serial Killer," Alexmanderson.com, May 28, 2014, http://www.alexmanderson.com/liu-pengli-the-first-serial-killer/.

6. Andrew Amelinckx, "Old Time Farm Crime: The Werewolf of Bedburg," Modern Farmer, August 5, 2013, http://modernfarmer.com/2013/08/peter-stubbethe-werewolf-of-bedburg/.

7. Stephen Wagner, "The Werewolf of Bedburg," About.com/Entertainment, http://paranormal.about.com/od/werewolves/a/The-Werewolf-Of-Bedburg_2.htm.

8. Joy Wittenburg, *Crime and Culture in Early Modern Germany* (Charlottesville, VA: University of Virginia Press, 2012), https://books.google.com/

9. "Peter Niers," Martian Herald, http://www.martianherald.com/10-ghastly-serial-killers-history/page/4.

10. "Giles Garnier: The Werewolf of Dole," Werewolves.com, http://www.werewolves.com/gilles-garnier-the-werewolf-of-dole/.

11. Richard Cavendish, "Death of Countess Elizabeth Bathory," History Today, August 8, 2014, http://www.historytoday.com/richard-cavendish/death-countess-elizabeth-bathory.

12. "Elizabeth Bathory: The Blood Countess," Rejected Princesses, http://www.rejectedprincesses.com/princesses/elisabeth-bathory.

13. "Elizabeth Bathory, The Blood Countess," Scandalous Women, http://scandalouswoman.blogspot.com/2009/10/elizabeth-bathory-blood-countess.html.

14. "The Cruel and Bloody Reign of Chile's La Quintrala," The Lineup, http://www.the-line-up.com/la-quintrala/.

15. "La Quintrala: The Chilean She-Devil," SJHStrangeTales.com, April 21, 2015, https://sjhstrangetales.wordpress.com/2015/04/21/la-quintrala-the-chilean-she-devil/.

16. "Aqua Tofana: Slow-Poisoning and Husband-Killing in 17th Century Italy," All Kinds of History, April 6, 2015, https://allkindsofhistory.wordpress.com/2015/04/06/aqua-tofana-slow-poisoning-and-husband-killing-in-17th-century-italy/.

17. "The Deadly Elixir of Giulana Tofana," The Lineup, http://www.the-line-up.com/giulia-tofana/.
18. "La Voisin," NNDB, http://www.nndb.com/people/875/000094593/.
19. "Catherine Deshayes," Murderpedia, http://murderpedia.org/female.D/d/deshayes-catherine.htm.
20. Tatiana Klevantseva, "Prominent Russians: Darya Saltykova," Russiapedia, http://russiapedia.rt.com/prominent-russians/history-and-mythology/darya-saltykova/.
21. Dr. Rebecca Tortello, "Lewis Hutchinson: The Mad Master," Pieces of the Past, http://old.jamaica-gleaner.com/pages/history/story0036.htm.
22. "Thug Behram: Famous Serial Killers," HellHorror.com, http://hellhorror.com/serial-killer-67/Thug-Behram.html.
23. "Thug Behram," FindTheData, http://serial-killers.findthedata.com/l/217/Thug-Behram.
24. Kathy Weiser, "The Vicious Harpes: First American Serial Killers," Legends of America, Updated January 2013, http://www.legendsofamerica.com/we-harpes.html.
25. "The Notorious Patty Cannon," Murder by Gaslight, December 14, 2013, http://www.murderbygaslight.com/2013/12/the-notorious-patty-cannon.html.
26. "The Notorious Patty Cannon," Genealogy Trails, http://genealogytrails.com/del/sussex/historypatty_cannon.html.
27. Adam Ruck, "The Serial Killer Hoteliers," France on Two Wheels, http://www.france2wheels.com/route-2-up-the-upper-allier-down-the-upper-loire/the-serial-killer-hoteliers/.
28. "Andreas Bichel," Murderpedia, http://murderpedia.org/male.B/b/bichel-andreas.htm.
29. "1809: Andreas Bichel, Bavarian Ripper," ExecutedToday.com, June 9, 2013, http://www.executedtoday.com/2013/06/09/1809-andreas-bichel-bavarian-ripper/.
30. "The Horrid and True Story of Burke and Hare," The Worlds of Burke and Hare, http://burkeandhare.com/.

31. "William Hare," Murderpedia, http://murderpedia.org/male.H/h/hare-william.htm.

32. "Helene Jegado," The Body Report, December 16, 2011, http://bodyreport.com/article/profile-helene-jegado.

33. "Gloomy Sunday: Hélène Jégado, French Serial Poisoner," Hedy: Stories About Noncomformist Women, http://hedymag.com/gloomy-sunday-helene-jegado-french-serial-poisoner/.

34. "The Werewolf of Allariz," Werewolves.com, http://www.werewolves.com/the-werewolf-of-allariz/.

35. "Manuel Blanco Romasanta," Murderpedia, http://murderpedia.org/male.B/b/blanco-romasanta.htm.

36. Allan Bellows, "Liver-Eating Johnson," Damn Interesting, January 22, 2006, http://www.damninteresting.com/liver-eating-johnson/.

37. "John Liver Eating Johnston," JohnLiverEatingJohnston.com, http://www.johnlivereatingjohnston.com/.

38. "H.H. Holmes," Bio, http://www.biography.com/people/hh-holmes-307622.

39. John Bartlow Martin, "The Master of Murder Castle," *Harper's Magazine*, December 1943, http://harpers.org/archive/1943/12/the-master-of-the-murder-castle/2/.

40. Martin Hill Ortiz, "The Twenty Seven Murders of Henry H. Holmes," A Predatory Mind, 2013, http://www.apredatorymind.com/The_Twenty_Seven_Murders_of_HH_Holmes_part_2.html.

41. "Jack the Ripper 1888," JacktheRipper.org, http://www.jack-the-ripper.org/.

42. "The Bender Family," Murderpedia, http://murderpedia.org/male.B/b/bender-family.htm.

43. "The Bloody Benders: America's First Serial Killers," Mental Floss, November 14, 2013, http://mentalfloss.com/article/53672/bloody-benders-americas-first-serial-killers.

44. "Earle Leonard Nelson," CrimeZZZ.net, http://www.crimezzz.net/serialkillers/N/NELSON_earle_leonard.php.

45. Troy Taylor, "Albert Fish: The Life & Crimes of One of America's Most Deranged Killers," Dead Men Do Tell Tales, 2004, http://www.prairieghosts.com/fish.html.

Glossary

arsenic—A metallic element that forms a number of poisonous compounds; used in insecticides and weed killers.

autopsy—Also known as a postmortem examination; a highly specialized surgical procedure that consists of a thorough examination of a corpse to determine the cause and manner of death and to evaluate any disease or injury that may be present.

black arts—Magic involving the supposed invocation of evil spirits for evil purposes.

bludgeon—To beat someone repeatedly with a heavy object.

conscience—An inner feeling or voice viewed as acting as a guide to the rightness or wrongness of one's behavior.

corpse—A dead body, especially of a human rather than an animal.

cyanide—A deadly type of poison.

exhume—To dig out something buried, especially a corpse from the ground.

masochism—The tendency to derive pleasure, especially sexual gratification, from one's own pain or humiliation.

odious—Extremely unpleasant or repulsive.

perversion—Sexual behavior or desire that is considered abnormal or unacceptable.

psychiatry—The study and treatment of mental illness, emotional disturbance, and abnormal behavior.

psychology—The scientific study of the human mind and its functions, especially those affecting behavior in a given context.

psychopath—A person suffering from a chronic mental disorder with abnormal or violent social behavior.

sadism—The tendency to derive pleasure, especially sexual gratification, from inflicting pain, suffering, or humiliation on others.

sadomasochism—Psychological tendency or sexual practice characterized by both sadism and masochism.

sociopath—A person with a personality disorder manifesting itself in extreme antisocial attitudes and behavior and a lack of conscience.

sternum—The breastbone.

supplicant—A fervently religious person who prays to God for help with a problem, or it can also be someone who begs earnestly for something he or she wants.

Further Reading

Books

Houck, Max M. and Jay A. Siegel. *Fundamentals of Forensic Science*. San Diego, CA: Academic Press/Elsevier, 2015.

Lightning Guide Editors. *Serial Killers: Jack the Ripper to the Zodiac Killer*. Berkeley, CA: Lightning Guides/Callisto Media, 2015.

Parker, R.J. *The Serial Killer Compendium*. Seattle: CreateSpace Independent Publishing, 2012.

Ronson, Jan. *The Psychopath Test: A Journey Through the Madness Industry*. New York: Penguin Publishing, 2012.

Weston-Davies, Wynne. *The Real Mary Kelly: Jack the Ripper's Fifth Victim and the Identity of the Man That Killed Her*. London, England: Blink Publishing, 2016.

Websites

Murderpedia
www.murderpedia.org
Murderpedia is the world's largest database of serial killers.

The Serial Killer Database Research Project
skdb.fgcu.edu/info.asp
The Serial Killer Database Research Project collects data on serial killers and presents public statistics.

Videos

The Mind of a Murderer. Investigation Discovery. 2015.

Index